GW01066339

Financial Policy and
Central Banking in Japan

Financial Policy and
Central Banking in Japan

Thomas F. Cargill
Michael M. Hutchison
Takatoshi Ito

The MIT Press
Cambridge, Massachusetts
London, England

This book was set in Palatino in QuarkXPress by Asco Typesetters, Hong Kong, and was printed and bound in the United States of America.

Library of Congress Cataloging-in-Publication Data

Cargill, Thomas F.
  Financial policy and central banking in Japan / Thomas F. Cargill, Michael M. Hutchison, and Takatoshi Ito.
      p.   cm.
  Includes bibliographical references and index.
  ISBN 0-262-03285-6 (hc. : alk. paper)
    1. Finance—Japan. 2. Banks and banking, Central—Japan. I. Hutchison, Michael M.
  II. Ito, Takatoshi, 1950– III. Title.
  HG187.J3 C368   2000
  332.1'1'0952—dc21   00-041813

Contents

Preface

Our collaboration on this book began shortly before The MIT Press published our earlier book, *The Political Economy of Japanese Monetary Policy* in August 1997. That book focused on financial and monetary developments in Japan from the end of World War II to the November 1996 Big Bang announcement of financial liberalization. We knew during the production of the first book the new Bank of Japan Law would be introduced shortly and started to plan a short sequel. We did not realize at the time, however, that a major economic and financial drama would unfold in Japan during the last three years of the 1990s. The near meltdown of Japan's financial system and serious recession forced a restructuring of Japan's financial and monetary institutions that will continue well into the new century. This book presents both a positive and normative analysis of how Japan has begun the process of shifting from an "old" to a "new" financial and central banking regime.

The authors have enjoyed the collaborative work on this book which was accomplished in many places as their itineraries crossed. Meetings took place in Osaka and Tokyo, Japan; Reno, Nevada; Berkeley and Santa Cruz, California; and, Sydney, Australia.

The authors have benefited from numerous interactions with individuals and institutions over the past three years in the preparation of this book. They would especially like to express appreciation to Mitsuhiro Fukao, Patricia Kuwayama, Kunio Okina, Yuri Okina, Hugh Patrick, Shigenori Shiratsuka, Naoyuki Yoshino, and reviewers of the first draft of this book. Their assistance and encouragement combined with help from institutions mentioned below contributed importantly to the book.

Cargill especially thanks the Bank of Japan, Keio University, University of Hawaii, Program on International Financial Systems at the Harvard Law School, and the International Monetary Fund for providing a forum to present many of the issues discussed in this book. Cargill acknowledges financial support from the Japan–U.S. Friendship Commission. He also expresses appreciation to students who read and commented on a draft of the book used in several courses, especially Jane Cook. Hutchison especially thanks the Center for Pacific Basin Monetary and Economic Studies at the Federal Reserve Bank of San Francisco. They have provided a stimulating research environment to study Japanese financial and central banking issues. Hutchison also acknowledges research support from the Social Sciences Division and the Committee on Research at the University of California at Santa Cruz; the International Center for the Study of East Asian Development, Kitakyushu; and the Pacific Rim Research Program of the University of California. Ito especially thanks the Institute of Economic Research at Hitotsubashi University and the National Bureau of Economic Research for providing a research and discussion forum for many of the issues discussed in this book. Ito joined the Ministry of Finance as Deputy Vice Minister for International Affairs in July 1999, but most of his contribution to this book was accomplished before he joined the Ministry, and no privileged information was used for this project.

Any opinions and viewpoints expressed in this book are those of the three authors alone, and not necessarily those of the institutions where they are currently or were previously associated.

1   Introduction

1.1   Lost Economic and Financial Development Opportunities in the 1990s

The 1990s turned out to be a traumatic decade for Japan. The economy experienced a long spell of stagnation and five quarters of declining output from 1997:4 to 1998:4. The unemployment rate soared while the inflation rate declined to zero and, in 1998, the economy came to the verge of a deflationary cycle. Economic, financial, and political instability dominated Japan and created a sense of uncertainty as the country faced the new century. Economic and financial distress were also accompanied by political instability as the public lost confidence in the government's ability to solve the growing problems. The 1990s may now be referred to as Japan's "lost decade" in terms of economic and financial development. One would have to go back to the late 1920s to find a similarly chaotic situation in Japan's peacetime history.

The economic, financial and political situation stabilized in late 1998 and 1999 as the economy's decline slowed and a tentative recovery began with positive real GDP growth in the first two quarters of 1999. The "Japan premium," which represents the additional cost of overnight borrowing by Japanese banks in the international market, disappeared by April 1999, following the government's action to recapitalize the banking system for a second time in March 1999. Although the economy contracted somewhat in the second half of 1999, real GDP for the year overall was slightly higher than 1998. The somewhat improved economic environment was accompanied by aggressive restructuring of the financial and real sector as well as changes in government institutions and attitudes about market forces. The more aggressive approach to dealing with troubled financial institutions, continued financial liberalization, and more expansionary fiscal and monetary policy set the foundation for a return to sustained economic and financial development in Japan.

The collapse of equity prices in the 1990 to 1992 period, and the decade-long decline in land prices, are the proximate causes of the stagnation and instability of the 1990s. However, more fundamental causes are rooted in Japan's approach to financial regulation and management of the economy. A series of financial, fiscal, and monetary policy failures delayed both economic recovery and resolution of the financial distress that had gradually built to crisis proportions by the second half of the decade. Accumulation of nonperforming loans pushed many financial institutions towards bankruptcy and took Japan to the edge of a financial panic in November 1997 with the failures of Hokkaido Takushoku Bank and Yamaichi Securities Company. The failure of these two large institutions challenged the basic principle of Japan's financial system based on mutual support and a policy of no failures of large institutions. It was now clear that no bank or institution was too large to fail in Japan.

The growing banking crisis from 1991 to 1997 was accompanied by economic stagnation and almost no growth. The economic situation sharply worsened in late 1997, after some signs of a recovery in 1996. Output declined at an alarming rate in late 1997 and 1998 and unemployment rose to 4.9 percent, the highest level recorded in modern Japan. The situation was further exacerbated by the sudden emergence of economic and financial problems in a number of Asian economies. Capital flight, currency depreciation, banking problems, and recession spread from Thailand to many of the other East Asian economies in late 1997, including South Korea. The crisis in the region affected Japan through its close trade and investment linkages. Moreover the East Asian financial systems resembled their Japanese counterpart, in that the banking system as opposed to capital markets, played a major role in channeling high savings to domestic investment. As a result the Asian crisis brought more critical attention to Japan's economic and financial structure, particularly since Japan had provided the model for much of postwar Asia.

The international concern with world economic and financial stability in 1998 had not been so intense since the 1930s. While not related to Japan's and Asia's problems, the devaluation of the ruble and the Russian government's default on its internal debt in August 1998 and the currency problems that emerged in Brazil in late 1998, added to the concern about a worldwide financial panic. Policy makers recognized the differences that existed between the 1920s to 1930s and the 1990s, but nonetheless, the financial and economic events of 1998 rekindled memories of the collapse of the international financial system in the 1930s and the associated economic and political instability. Japan, as the second-largest economy in the world and a key element of the international financial system, was the focus of international policy discussions.

Economic and financial distress in Japan in 1998 was accompanied by political instability. The Liberal Democratic Party (LDP) lost its long-held postwar majority in the Lower House in 1993. The LDP for two years was the majority opposition party, but regained the majority in 1996. However, amid a deteriorating economy and scandals at the Ministry of Finance and the Bank of Japan, the LDP failed to win a majority in the Upper House election July 1998 and Prime Minister Hashimoto shortly thereafter resigned. The loss in the Upper House was a serious blow to the LDP. The Upper House elections occur every three years and do not usually attract the degree of attention as elections for the Lower House. The Lower House is a far more important political institution and elections for the Lower House must be called within a four-year period. Nonetheless, Japanese voters came out in record numbers to register their displeasure. Japanese leadership was thus faced with its most serious challenge in five decades. The Japanese public's confidence in the government bureaucracy was shaken.

Thus economic and political factors combined to provide strong incentives for the new Prime Minister, Keizo Obuchi, to take unprecedented action. The economic, financial, and political situation stabilized in late 1998 and 1999, especially after the injection of massive public money into major banks in March 1999. Japan faces many challenges in the new century, but the foundation for recovery and sustained economic and financial development was finally established by the end of the 1990s.

1.2 Economic and Financial Distress Signals a Turning Point in Japan's Postwar Economy

The performance of the Japanese economy in the 1990s stands in sharp contrast to the economic, financial, and political stability that characterized Japan since the start of reconstruction in 1950. The economic and financial performance record to the late 1980s for the most part was impressive by any standard.

Cargill, Hutchison, and Ito (1997) reviewed and analyzed Japan's economic and financial performance from 1945 to late 1996, ending with the November 1996 announcement of the "Big Bang" approach to financial reform. The Big Bang established an agenda to bring greater competitiveness, efficiency, and international involvement and openness to the financial system and regulatory structure. The objective of the Big Bang was to transform Japan's financial system to equal London and New York by 2001. In hindsight, the Big Bang announcement in the midst of financial distress illustrated an unwillingness of the government to recognize the seriousness of the accumulating financial distress and recognize that past policies were incompatible with the new environment. The Big Bang agenda was an important and bold development. However, the bold vision for financial liberalization stood in contrast to the failure to deal aggressively with long-standing financial problems.

The roots of the financial crisis were set in the "bubble economy" of the later part of the 1980s characterized by rapid asset price inflation and a booming real sector. Structural characteristics of the banking system tied equity price increases to increased bank lending, thereby supporting a cumulative upward process in both prices and bank lending. Accommodative monetary policy, attempting to limit yen appreciation against a background of low consumer price inflation, inadvertently provided liquidity that accommodated asset inflation.

The Bank of Japan, in opposition to the Ministry of Finance, raised the discount rate in May 1989 from 2.5 to 3.5 percent. The discount rate was increased over the next fifteen months to 6.0 percent. Real estate companies were also subjected to lending limits in March 1990. Tighter monetary policy was instrumental in bursting the bubble and asset prices sharply declined. The Nikkei 225 Index peaked on the last trading day of 1989 and declined by over 50 percent during the next 18 months. Land and real estate prices started to fall in 1991 and continued to decline for most of the decade.

The subsequent decline in economic growth and asset prices revealed fundamental weaknesses in Japan's financial system but more importantly, revealed fundamental weaknesses in Japan's financial supervision and regulation framework. Failures in financial policy to resolve the nonperforming loan problem allowed financial distress to increase and reach a point that, by late 1997 and 1998, policy makers inside and outside of Japan were increasingly concerned that Japan's problems would spread to the rest of the world.

In Japan, financial distress was made worse by declining real output in late 1997 and 1998 and declining confidence of the Japanese people in the ability of their government to reverse the economic decline. A series of announced fiscal stimulus packages and seemingly easy monetary policy failed to revive the economy. Considerable debate ensued over whether the policies were as stimulative as advertised. Japan's bank problems and price deflation in the late 1990s were increasingly compared to the (much greater) problems experienced by many industrial economies in the 1930s. The apparent emergence of a "liquidity trap" in Japan, limiting the ability of the Bank of Japan to stimulate the economy brought similar comparisons. No industrial economy since the 1930s had experienced near-zero interest rates and expectations of declining prices[1]. Although the magnitude of GDP and price declines was quite different between Japan in the 1990s and the United States in the 1930s, the qualitative features were similar.

This book focuses on the events since the mid-1990s, tracing how the economic and financial situation deteriorated, analyzing the government response to the financial crisis, and addressing challenges facing financial and monetary policy in the years to come. The focus is on financial and central bank policy. We investigate how policy initially failed to deal with economic and financial distress, and how policy and institutions were redesigned to set the stage for a return to sustained economic and financial development.

1.3   Organization of the Book

In chapter 2 we discuss the events in late 1997 and 1998 that brought Japan to the edge of financial panic. The real sector was either stagnant or experiencing declining output for much of the 1990s. The financial sector had deteriorated to such a point by late 1997, that financial collapse was a serious concern. These events forced the Japanese government to recognize that its initial financial and monetary policy response, institutional changes in the structure of supervision and regulation, and revision of the 1942 Bank of Japan Law were insufficient. More fundamental changes were required to deal with the economic and financial problems. Chapter 2 places the 1997 crisis in the perspec-

---

1. Switzerland had negative interest rates in the 1960s to curb capital inflows.

tive of a longer-term process of financial and monetary development in postwar Japan and considers Japan's financial problems from an international perspective.

The "old" financial supervision and regulatory framework and the transition to a "new" framework are discussed in chapter 3. The old framework deserves credit for supporting Japan's impressive record of economic growth from 1950 to the mid-1980s. On the negative side, however, the structural imbalances and rigidities of the old system contributed to the economic and financial distress of the 1990s. We focus on a series of events since the mid-1990s that convinced Japanese policy makers, and the general public, that the old framework was incompatible with the new environment and incapable of dealing with the financial distress. The new framework consists of new institutions such as the Financial Supervisory Agency and the Financial Reconstruction Commission and reorganized institutions such as the Deposit Insurance Corporation, Bank of Japan, and the Ministry of Finance. More important, the new framework incorporates new attitudes about market forces, competition, and the role of government supervision and regulation. The chapter ends with a discussion of the role of the Bank of Japan in the new financial supervision and regulation framework.

In chapter 4 we discuss the revision of the 1942 Bank of Japan Law and the characteristics of the "new" Bank of Japan Law. The new Bank of Japan Law is placed in historical context to understand why the Bank of Japan was permitted to operate under a "wartime" version of the Law until March 31, 1998, and the events that led to revision of the Law in June 1997. Using established methods to measure formal or legal independence, we evaluate how the new Bank of Japan Law has affected its legal independence.

The institutional redesign of the Bank of Japan is not an isolated event from an international perspective. The new Bank of Japan reflects a general process of central bank redesign that has been in process during the past decade. In chapter 5, therefore, we review the arguments in favor of central bank institutional design that provides legal independence from the government. While these issues are discussed from a broad perspective, the chapter discusses these issues in the context of Bank of Japan policy and the specific problems faced by the new Bank of Japan in the late 1990s. We argue that there is a strong case for the Bank of Japan to adopt an inflation target as a framework of conducting monetary policy.

Chapter 6 discusses the challenges faced by Japanese policy makers in managing the financial and monetary system. This chapter covers a variety of issues, some short term in nature, but most of long term significance. We analyze Japan's attempts to transform its financial and monetary institutions to simultaneously deal with the economic and financial crisis of the 1990s and establish a foundation for sustained economic and financial development. This chapter offers insights into Japan's prospects for achieving these goals.

2

The 1990s: Unprecedented Economic and Financial Distress

2.1 Introduction

Economic and financial distress in Japan in the 1990s had no precedent since the end of postwar reconstruction, and also stands out as a period of instability compared with much of prewar Japan. Financial distress, however, was qualitatively and quantitatively more serious than the adverse effects on the real economy. The real impact is reflected by weak real GDP performance (figure 2.1) throughout the 1990s. The economy stagnated in the early 1990s, with real GDP growth barely above zero, exhibited positive GDP growth from 1995 through late 1997 that sharply turned negative in late 1997. After five quarters of falling output, the economy rebounded and grew in the first two quarters of 1999 but again declined in the second half of the year. Real GDP in 1999 nevertheless was slightly higher than 1998. While Japan's economic growth in the 1990s was weak, especially in comparison with the previous four decades, the real economy was not in a depression or collapsing situation.

Financial distress was far more serious. Japan's financial system had problems throughout the decade, but a state of near panic occurred in late 1997 and early 1998. The magnitude of financial distress, measured in terms of either nonperforming loans (10 to 20 percent of GDP) or insolvent institutions, was large. Moreover policy errors in dealing with the financial crisis throughout most of the decade revealed a fundamental flaw in Japan's approach to regulation and supervision of the financial system. Traditional policies were incompatible with the new economic, technological, and political environment.

This chapter reviews the economic and financial distress in the 1990s from six perspectives. First, we place the developments during

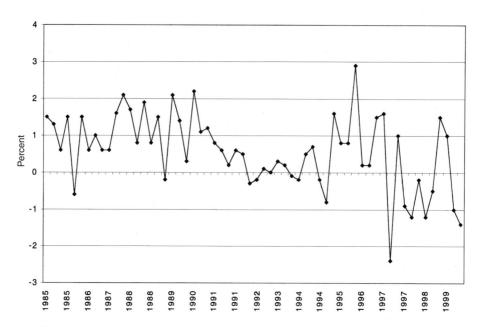

Figure 2.1
Real GDP growth: 1985 to 1999 quarter-to-quarter growth rates. Source: Economic Planning Agency (*www.epa.go.jp*).

the 1990s in the context of Japan's postwar financial and monetary experience. Second, we discuss the performance of the real economy and the role of fiscal and monetary policy in the 1990s. Third, we discuss how ongoing financial distress in the first half of the 1990s developed into a crisis in late 1997. Fourth, the role of government policy in bringing about the crisis is discussed. We show how market forces, reflected by the "Japan premium" on overnight borrowing by Japanese banks, revealed a sharp drop in confidence about the government's approach to resolving financial distress. Fifth, we discuss how the financial and economic problems in Japan shared common features with the crisis in Asia and other parts of the world that emerged in 1997 and 1998. While economic and financial distress in other parts of the world were not directly connected to Japan, it did elevate international concern and pressure for Japan to deal more aggressively with its own problems. Finally, we analyze whether financial distress in Japan was special compared to banking problems experienced by a large number of developed and developing countries in the late 1980s and 1990s.

2.2   The 1990s in Postwar Historical Perspective

Japan's economic, financial, and monetary development during the postwar period through the 1990s can be divided into six phases (Cargill, Hutchison, and Ito 1997). The six phases are defined and summarized in table 2.1. Each phase represents a distinct period of economic, financial, and monetary development in Japan, especially with respect to the evolution of financial and Bank of Japan policy.

Japan reached the "take off" stage by 1950 and, assisted by the positive economic effects of the Korean War, commenced a period of impressive economic growth accompanied by financial stability. Japan experienced moderate inflation until 1970 and relative price stability from 1975 to 1989. There were only two short periods of instability: the "wild inflation" and oil price shocks of the early 1970s and the dislocations caused by the second set of oil price shocks in 1979–80. The inflation of the early 1970s was effectively eliminated by monetary policy and, in the process, the Bank of Japan achieved a meaningful degree of political independence from the Ministry of Finance. The 1979–80 oil price shocks revealed a serious commitment to price stability. Unlike many other industrial countries, Japan did not attempt to offset the adverse effects of the oil price shocks by expansionary monetary growth. As a result Japan was able to avoid the high inflation rates of the early 1980s and subsequent decline in real economic activity experienced by many other industrialized economies as they were required to adopt restrictive monetary and fiscal policies to disinflate their economies. The primary responsibility for stabilization policy was placed on the Bank of Japan, while the Ministry of Finance focused on a gradual and sustained effort to reduce the central government deficit starting in the mid-1970s through the 1980s (Cargill and Hutchison, 1997)

Japan had established itself by 1985 as the world's second largest economy and largest creditor nation. There was every indication that Japan would continue to generate impressive economic performance. Problems emerged in the second half of the 1980s, however. While real GDP continued to grow in the 3 to 6 percent range, and inflation remained low, pressure on the banking and financial system was building. Land and equity prices after 1986 increased to levels that, in hindsight, could not be rationalized by economic fundamentals and led to Japan's characterization in the second half of the 1980s as the "bubble economy." The bubble economy followed the pattern of a

Table 2.1
Phase of economic and financial development in Japan: End of World War II to 1999

Phase I: End of World War to 1950

Postwar adjustment and establishment of a foundation for rapid growth	Economic and financial disruptions are manifested by triple digit inflation rates, government deficits, and excessive monetary growth.
	Dodge Plan commits government to balanced budget, lower monetary growth, and fixed exchange rate of 360 yen to the dollar.
	Inflation rate declines from 166 percent in 1948 to 18.2 percent in 1950 accompanied by sharp decline in output.

Phase II: 1950 to 1970

Period of high economic growth	Rapid real GDP growth averages about 10 percent per year, with moderate inflation of about 4.5 percent.
	Monetary policy is constrained by fixed exchange rate.
	Financial system is organized as an instrument of industrial policy, making it the most regulated and administratively controlled financial system among the industrial countries.
	Financial stability is attained without official failures of financial institutions, except for the government's efforts to bail out Yamaichi Securities in 1965.
	Monetary policy is adapted to the rigidly regulated financial structure and based on qualitative and quantitative credit controls.

Phase III: 1970 to 1975

"Wild inflation" caused by Bank of Japan excessive monetary growth, which in turn, resulted from political interference and higher priority placed on external than internal objectives	Economy is adversely affected by oil price increases, "Nixon" shocks, and yen appreciation as the fixed exchange rate system comes to an end by 1973.
	Monetary growth and inflation increase in 1971 and 1972 as Bank of Japan policy attempts to ensure high rates of real GDP growth and limit yen appreciation as the Bretton Woods System collapses.
	Inflation rises to double-digit rates in 1973 and in October 1973, OPEC imposes an oil embargo and sharp increases in oil prices follow and continue into 1974.
	Bank of Japan adopts a new policy focused on price stability.

Phase IV: 1975 to 1985

Sustained economic growth, price stability, and financial liberalization	Bank of Japan achieves considerable de facto independence because of previous opposition to expansionary monetary policy and adverse effects of "wild inflation."

Table 2.1 (continued)

	End of fixed exchange rate system permits Bank of Japan to focus on price stability and Bank of Japan announces money projections. Resulting monetary policy is nonmonetarist in rhetoric but monetarist in outcome.
	Financial liberalization commences and changes Bank of Japan operating environment.
	Bank of Japan shifts its emphasis from credit controls to an interest-rate focused policy.
	Financial liberalization is gradual and smooth; Japan experiences none of the financial disruptions that characterize other countries undergoing liberalization such as the United States, since the Bank of Japan's price stabilization policy keeps the gap between regulated and unregulated interests narrow.
	World attention is directed toward the Bank of Japan and Japan's approach to financial liberalization.
Phase V: 1985 to May 1989	
Bubble economy and asset inflation	Asset inflation after 1987 takes on characteristics of a speculative bubble; excessive monetary growth and structural characteristics of banking system ensure an upward cumulative process of equity and land prices.
	Second postwar mistake of monetary policy: higher priority placed on external (limiting yen appreciation) than internal (asset inflation) considerations.
	Overall inflation rate remains low until 1988 and 1989.
Phase VI: May 1989 to 1999	
Burst of the bubble economy, recession, financial distress, evidence of recovery and Big Bang announcement, edge of financial collapse, political instability, and hesitant recovery	Bank of Japan raises discount rate in May 1989 followed by more increases and tighter monetary policy.
	Collapse of equity prices in 1990 and 1991 generates recession. Land prices decline through the 1990s.
	Failures of small credit cooperatives and eventual market insolvency of Deposit Insurance Corporation. By 1995, a number of financial institutions including small banks have been declared insolvent.
	Government establishes institutions to assume responsibility for nonperforming loans (Cooperative Credit Purchasing Company in 1992, Resolution and Collection Bank in 1996, and the Housing Loan Administration in 1996).
	Government closes *jusen* or housing loan companies and reforms Deposit Insurance Corporation.

Table 2.1 (continued)

Economic and financial recovery appear to be taking hold in late 1995 and 1996.
Prime Minister Hashimoto announces Big Bang financial reforms as part of a platform of the newly elected LDP to reform the Japanese economy.
Inappropriate fiscal policy in 1997 contributes to economic slowdown.
Serious economic and financial downturn in late 1997 and 1998; public willing to use taxpayer funding to resolve nonperforming loan problem, but public losses confidence in ability of government to deal with growing economic and financial distress.
LDP losses majority in Upper House and Prime Minister Hashimoto resigns in July 1998.
New administration takes a more aggressive approach in dealing with troubled financial institutions and makes a larger commitment of public funding.
Simulative fiscal policy accompanied by hesitant Bank of Japan policy work at cross purposes. Despite potential problems with insufficiently aggressive monetary policy, economic and financial distress declines in 1999.

classic speculative bubble. The subsequent fall in asset prices in the early 1990s, initiated by an increase in the Bank of Japan discount rate in May 1989, and the subsequent recession, adversely impacted bank balance sheets.

Financial institutions were saddled with massive nonperforming loans estimated in late 1998 at between 10 to 20 percent of GDP. The banking crisis and nonperforming loan problem were exacerbated by regulatory inertia, forbearance, and forgiveness. The piecemeal and tentative approach initially followed by the Ministry of Finance in dealing with the banking crisis exhausted the limited resources of the Deposit Insurance Corporation without confronting the underlying weaknesses of the financial system. The Deposit Insurance Corporation is the larger and most important of the two government deposit insurance corporations in Japan, while the other corporation insures deposits of agricultural and fisheries cooperatives (Cargill, Hutchison, and Ito 1996).

A turning point appeared to be reached in 1995–96 when more decisive action was taken. The government closed the *jusen* or housing-loan industry, restructured the Deposit Insurance Corporation, and discussions began among the regulatory authorities to adopt more aggressive approaches to dealing with troubled financial institutions. Real GDP began to increase in late 1995 and 1996 suggesting recovery was in place and official estimates of nonperforming loans declined from 1995 to 1996. In November 1996 Prime Minister Ryutaro Hashimoto—at the head of a newly reorganized Liberal Democratic Party elected following a campaign heralding broad-based reform—announced an extensive deregulation of Japan's financial system by the year 2001. This proposal, announced as the directive of the Prime Minister to the Finance Minister, was likened by senior officials to the "Big Bang" financial deregulation in the United Kingdom in the 1980s. The far-reaching objective of the initiative was intended to launch a series of changes to make Tokyo a global financial center that would rival New York and London, working from three basic principles of reform: "market mechanism," "global nature," and "transparency."

The Diet passed legislation in spring and early summer 1997 in response to the initiative (Cargill, Hutchison, and Ito 1998). The new legislation, among other actions, created a new Financial Supervisory Agency, which greatly reduced the role of the Ministry of Finance in the monitoring and supervision of the financial system, deregulated the foreign exchange market, and revised the 1942 Bank of Japan Law.

The banking and general financial situation, however, deteriorated in late 1997 and brought Japan to a near-crisis situation. Japan's economy, for the first time since 1950, experienced falling real GDP, deflation, and market insolvency of large numbers of financial institutions. The paralysis characterizing Japan's financial system in the late 1990s affected all aspects of the Japanese economy. Mistakes in financial policy, especially failure to quickly resolve nonperforming loan and bank problems also weakened financial institutions and led to economic recession and stagnation for much of the decade. Concerns over the financial system fed pessimism about the economy in general, and the fall in confidence contributed to the deep and prolonged recession. The problem reached a crisis in November 1997, and led to a flurry of legislative actions designed to deal with insolvent financial institutions. These measures included a large commitment of public funds to protect depositors and recapitalize "solvent" financial institutions, creation of new institutions to take over the assets of failed banks, and political compromise allowing the temporary nationalization of the Long-Term Credit Bank of Japan and the Nippon Credit Bank.

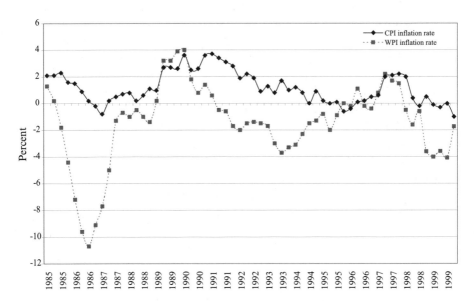

Figure 2.2
CPI and WPI inflation rate: 1985 to 1999. Annual growth rate calculated from the same quarter of the previous year to the current quarter. The growth rates of the CPI for the 1989:2 to 1990:1 and 1997:2 to 1998:1 period are biased upward by 3 and 2 percentage points, respectively, due to the introduction of a consumption tax in the first period and an increase in the consumption tax in the second period. Source: Statistics Bureau of the Management and Coordination Agency (*www.stat.go.jp*) for the CPI and the Bank of Japan (*www.boj.or.jp*) for the WPI.

2.3   The Real Economy and Macroeconomic Stabilization

Japan's economy stagnated from 1992 to 1994, exhibited a modest recovery in 1995 and 1996, and then sharply declined in 1997 and 1998. Real GDP grew only slightly (0.3 percent) in 1999. Japan's economic growth performance in the 1990s was the worst among the industrial countries. In terms of economic growth, the decade of the 1990s is arguably the worst peacetime decade of Japan since the start of industrialization in 1868.

Signs of deflation and stagnation were apparent. The inflation rate, measured by the Consumer Price Index, declined in the first half of the 1990s, rose slightly through the end of 1997, then became slightly negative in 1998 and 1999 (figure 2.2). The measured index, however, understates the degree of price deflation, since there is a well-known and substantial upward bias in the Consumer Price Index. The Whole-

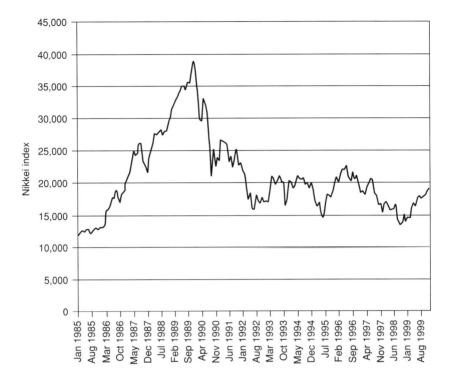

Figure 2.3
Nikkei 225 index end of month values: January 1985 to August 1999. Source: *Nihon Keizai Shinbun Company* (*www.nikkei.co.jp*).

sale Price Index, which is not subject to the same type or degree of upward bias, declined in 1991 and exhibited negative inflation rates throughout much of the decade (figure 2.2). With declining prices, the real GDP growth became negative from the fourth quarter of 1997 to the first quarter of 1999 (figure 2.1). Stagnation and decline were also exhibited in the stock market (figure 2.3), short- and long-term interest rates (figure 2.4), bank credit (figure 2.5), land prices (figure 2.6), and the unemployment rate (figure 2.7).

The poor real economic performance of the Japanese economy in the 1990s raises at least three questions. First, what caused the shift from high and sustained economic growth from 1950 to 1990, to stagnation and decline in the 1990s? Second, why did the sharp downturn take place in late 1997? Third, why were fiscal and monetary policies ineffective in stimulating the economy?

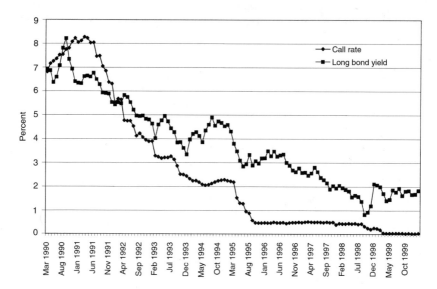

Figure 2.4
Short- and long-term interest rates: March 1990 to February 2000. Source: Call rate, uncollateralized overnight: Bank of Japan (*www.boj.or.jp*). Ordinary government bond yield, longest-term, Tokyo, OTC. Bank of Japan (*www.boj.or.jp*).

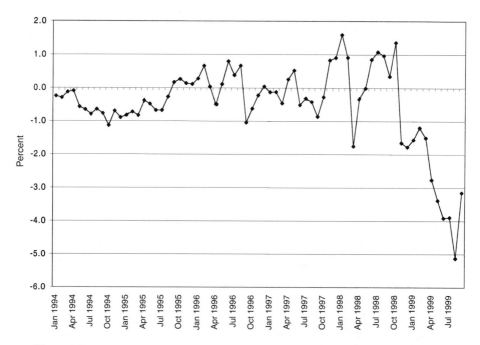

Figure 2.5
Bank lending growth rate: January 1994 to September 1999. Loans and discounts for all banks. Annual growth rate calculated from the same month of the previous year to the current month. Source: Japanese Bankers Association (*www.zenginkyo.or.jp*).

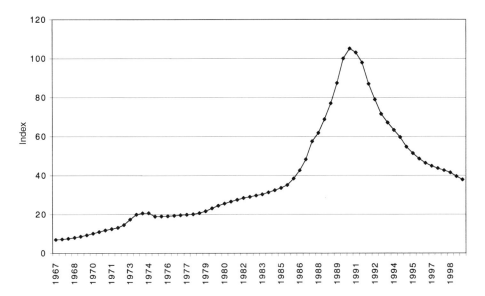

Figure 2.6
Urban land price index, six metropolitan cities, all purposes (residential, commercial, and industrial): 1967 to 1999. Source: Japan Real Estate Institute (*www.reinet.or.jp*).

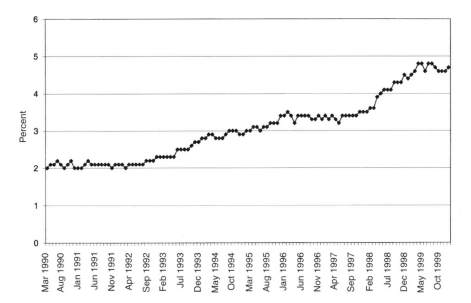

Figure 2.7
Unemployment rate: March 1990 to February 2000. Source: Statistics Bureau of the Management and Coordination Agency (*www.stat.go.jp*).

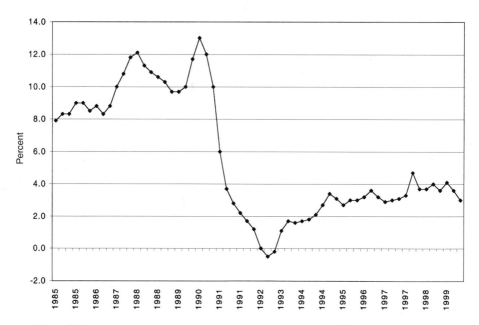

Figure 2.8
M2+CD money supply growth: 1985 to 1999. Annual growth rate calculated from
the same quarter of the previous year to the current month. Source: Bank of Japan
(*www.boj.or.jp*).

The proximate cause of economic decline in the early 1990s was
the collapse of asset prices in 1991 and 1992 and restrictive monetary
policy. The underlying cause, however, was the inevitability of a collapse in the extraordinary Japanese bubble economy of the late 1980s.
The collapse of asset prices generated a negative wealth effect on
spending and investment, led to a decline in consumer confidence, and
deteriorated balance sheets of banks and other financial institutions as
the market value of collateral and the ability to service debt declined.
Lending by commercial banks declined. The economic decline was also
the result of the slowdown in business investment from the high rates
of investment in the latter 1980s.

The specific timing of the collapse of asset prices was related, in part,
to the restrictive monetary policy initiated May 1989 by the Bank of
Japan when it raised the official discount rate from 2.5 to 3.5 percent.
The discount was increased four more times to 6.0 percent August
1990. The growth of M2+CDs subsequently declined and became negative in late 1992 and early 1993 (figure 2.8).

Monetary policy shifted to expansion after early 1993 as measured by the growth of M2 + CDs. The discount rate had been reduced earlier starting in July 1991 when the rate was reduced from 6.0 to 5.5 percent. The discount rate was reduced in stages until it reached 0.5 percent in September 1995, and it has remained at this level through 1999. In addition to monetary stimulus, the government implemented a series of fiscal packages to stimulate the economy. Economic and financial distress eased, and by 1996 there was evidence that recovery in both the real and financial sectors was beginning to take hold.

The recovery, however, was short-lived, for the economy sharply declined in late 1997. The sharp downturn is related to a fiscal tightening and then a "credit crunch" associated with the deteriorating situation of the banking industry. An increase in the consumption tax rate from 3 to 5 percent, combined with an end to a temporary income tax cut in April 1997, amounted to a tax increase of 9 trillion yen.

The fiscal contraction was compounded by credit contraction on the part of bad-debt-ridden banks. Banks were under pressure to increase their risk-adjusted capital ratio to meet the international BIS (Bank for International Settlements) standard established in 1988. The BIS standards require that banks with international operations maintain an 8 percent capitalization for risk-weighted assets. Riskless assets such as government bonds are excluded from the asset base, while commercial loans are counted as risky assets. Capital is classified into equity (tier I capital) and other assets close to capital (tier II capital) such as subordinated debt or in the case of Japan, 45 percent of the unrealized gains or "latent" gains on equity holdings. Of the 8 percent ratio of capital to risk-weighted assets, 4 percent must be in the form of tier I capital.

Continued nontransparency by banks regarding the true size of nonperforming loans only heightened suspicion among investors and made it difficult for banks to issue stock or subordinate debt. Asset reduction was the only remaining measure by which banks could improve their capital asset ratios and meet the BIS standard. Ito and Sasaki (1998) found that the BIS requirements had a significant portfolio allocation effect on Japanese banks as equity prices declined and reduced latent capital gains. The BIS capital requirements contributed importantly to reduced bank lending.

The deterioration of the financial system resumed with the failures of Hokkaido Takushoku and Yamaichi Securities. While official estimates of nonperforming loans declined from 50 trillion yen in March

1995 to 32 trillion yen in March 1996, revised estimates of nonperforming loans with new and broader definitions increased the estimate
of nonperforming loans to 60 trillion yen in March 1997. Unofficial estimates placed the total size of nonperforming loans by year-end 1998 at
between 60 and 100 trillion yen (10 to 20 percent of GDP).

The causes of the economic and financial collapse in the early 1990s
and of the sharp downturn in late 1997 are fairly clear. Monetary
policy contributed to asset inflation in the second half of the 1980s,
and the inevitable burst of the bubble brought on economic and financial distress. In this case, the burst of the bubble was preceded and
perhaps precipitated by the Bank of Japan's tightening policy in May
1989. The sharp downturn in late 1997, by contrast, was influenced by
the consumption tax increase.

In broad perspective, however, the 1990s have been the subject of
much discussion and debate over whether poor economic performance
was primarily attributable to macroeconomic or structural factors. If
macroeconomic, the question is whether fiscal and/or monetary policy
were sufficiently stimulative.

A number of observers (e.g., Posen 1998, 1999; Weinstein 2000) argue
that the poor performance of the Japanese economy in the 1990s is
more the outcome of standard macroeconomic shocks and insufficient
aggregate demand than structural problems that manifest themselves
through aggregate supply. Posen, for example, presents a convincing
case that fiscal policy, despite official claims, added little on balance to
aggregate demand until the stimulus packages enacted in 1998. The fiscal action in 1997 was clearly restrictive, and there was ample evidence
to suggest that Japan would have benefited if fiscal packages had included more tax relief than spending.

Posen, as well as the authors of this book, argue that monetary policy was not as expansionary as conditions warranted in the second half
of the 1990s. A lively debate developed between Bank of Japan officials, including Okina (1999a, 1999b, 1999c) and Ueda (1999a, 1999b),
and outsiders (McKinnon 1999; Meltzer 1999) over Bank of Japan
policy. This debate will be addressed more fully in chapters 5 and 6.

No doubt mistakes were made with both fiscal and monetary policy.
At the same time serious structural problems also permeated Japan's
economy. These structural problems included a corporate governance
system unresponsive to equity holders, large nonperforming loans,
and the absence of an infrastructure to dispose of bad loans. Moreover
other weaknesses included institutions and regulation that tied equity

and land price performance to bank performance, and a deposit guarantee system based on mutual support that was beset by moral hazard. As a practical matter, however, there is a serious identification problem in any attempt to separate the two causal explanations for understanding Japan's weak economy in the 1990s. It is likely that both policy errors by the government (fiscal, financial regulation, and monetary policy) and structural problems, especially those associated with financial regulation and the structure of financial markets, bear responsibility.

2.4 Edge of Financial Panic: November 1997

Japan experienced a near-banking crisis in November 1997 when two large financial institutions failed. The Hokkaido Takushoku Bank (also referred to as *Takugin*), a large regional bank and Yamaichi Securities Company, fourth largest of the Big Four securities firms in Japan both failed in November 1997. The failure of these two institutions was preceded a few weeks by the failure of Sanyo Securities Company—a much smaller securities firm than Yamaichi. Although smaller financial institutions had been failing, and depleting the deposit insurance fund since 1991, the failures of Sanyo and especially, Hokkaido Takushoku and Yamaichi raised concern that financial distress had reached the center of Japan's financial system. Hokkaido Takushoku and Yamaichi were qualitatively and quantitatively different because of their size and, in the case of Yamaichi, international operations.

Sanyo Surprise

The crisis of November 1997 started with the failure of Sanyo Securities, a middle-sized securities firm. On November 3, Sanyo Securities filed for protection from creditors (equivalent of chapter 11 bankruptcy in the United States). The failure raised concern for three reasons. First, it was an established securities firm that failed from bad investment decisions, providing a window on the seriousness of the problems likely facing other institutions. Second, Sanyo was not "rescued" by the usual procedure involving a merger to a healthy financial institution. This showed the limitation of government intervention as well as the limited resources in the industry itself. Third, Sanyo defaulted on some of its call loans (interbank short-term loans) after receiving legal protection from its creditors.

Retail customers' assets in the Sanyo Securities were protected because of their theoretical and legal separation from the companies' assets. Nonetheless, the failure created among investors a general sense of concern over the fragility of Japanese securities firms. Sanyo was the first case in Japan where a financial institution had filed for bankruptcy protection from creditors, as opposed to a rescue merger (as had occurred in many cases) or an outright liquidation (e.g., Hanwa Bank). Sanyo's default in the interbank call market was also unprecedented for an institution of its size and stature.

Hokkaido Takushoku

Sanyo's default contributed to the failure of Hokkaido Takushoku which announced on November 17 that it would sell some of its assets to other banks and would be liquidated within a year. Its failure came as a surprise since the Ministry of Finance had publicly pledged to protect the large banks in Japan of which Hokkaido Takushoku was included under its "too big to fail" policy. The policy was announced in 1995 when the Deposit Insurance Corporation was recapitalized after the Corporation's funds had been exhausted by failures of small credit cooperatives. Hokkaido Takushoku was the most significant failure of a financial institution representative of the most important part of Japan's financial system since the start of reindustrialization in 1950.

Rumors about the problems at Hokkaido Takushoku had circulated since at least mid-1997. On April 1, 1997, Hokkaido Takushoku announced a merger plan with the Hokkaido Bank—one of the 60-some regional banks and standing next to the big-20 in size. The merger would take place with some restructuring, such as a complete withdrawal from abroad and consolidation of the branch networks. The merger target date was set to be on April 1, 1998. Since both banks were plagued with large nonperforming loans, the merit of the merger was to come from consolidating branch networks that competed heavily in the Hokkaido prefecture. However, the merger talks did not go smoothly, and this became common knowledge over the summer. It was formally announced in mid-September that the merger process would be "postponed indefinitely." Hokkaido Takushoku started to withdraw from its international operations by shutting down foreign branch offices. Large-scale deposit withdrawals began in the summer and continued into November. Loss of deposits combined with the credit squeeze in the interbank call market after the Sanyo default made it increasingly difficult for Hokkaido Takushoku to raise funds.

On Friday, November 14, Hokkaido Takushoku experienced the unusual problem of securing sufficient funds in the call market to settle its transactions balance for the day. Getting close to outright default, bank management decided to suspend operations. After intensive discussion with the Ministry of Finance and the Bank of Japan over the weekend, Hokkaido Takushoku on Monday (November 17) announced the following actions: (1) Hokkaido Takushoku would sell the good assets and liabilities of its branch network in Hokkaido to the Hokuyo Bank, (2) the branch network in regions outside Hokkaido (mostly in Tokyo) would be sold, (3) bad assets would be sold to the Resolution and Collection Bank originally established in 1996 to assume assets of failed credit cooperatives, and (4) the Bank of Japan would provide the loans needed for liquidity support (deposit protection).

The stock market had reacted to the Sanyo Securities failure by pushing down the stock prices of the weaker financial institutions in Japan. The stock prices of Hokkaido Takushoku, Yamaichi Securities, Yasuda Trust Bank, and Nippon Credit Bank, among others, dropped markedly. By contrast, on the day that the Hokkaido Takushoku failure was announced, stock prices soared—the Nikkei 225 index jumped by 1,200 yen—reportedly because of the expectation that the government would be prompted to set out guidelines for using public money to deal with similar bank failures. This expectation was dashed, however, when Prime Minister Hashimoto presented a very negative view towards using public funds to help liquidate, restructure or recapitalize problem banks.

Yamaichi Failure

One week after the failure of Hokkaido Takushoku, Yamaichi also failed—the third collapse of the month—and also surprised many observers because of its status as one of the Big Four securities firms. The losses at Yamaichi had also been rumored for several months. Yamaichi had shifted accumulated unrealized losses to subsidiaries and omitted them from its own balance sheet. In order to hide losses, for example, Yamaichi resorted to selling securities to clients during the current accounting period at inflated prices with buy-back guarantees effective during future accounting periods. These tactics only delayed its demise and increased Yamaichi losses since stock prices did not recover. When rumors of Yamaichi's practice surfaced, its stock price plummeted, and credit lines in the call market to the company were cut.

2.5   The Japan Premium, Scandals, and Government Response

The failures of these institutions in November 1997 prompted a sense that no institution was immune from failure despite a government blanket guarantee of all deposits to March 2001 that had been announced by the Ministry of Finance in late 1995. The failure of Hokkaido Takushoku, though it did not involve depositor losses, further weakened the government's credibility because the government had assured the public that the financial problems were largely confined to smaller financial institutions. Economists and policy observers outside of Japan were also alarmed by the failure of Yamaichi because the failure of a large internationally active institution raised the risk of spillovers to other countries through the payments system and money market.

International risk was minimal in the failures of Sanyo Securities and Hokkaido Takushoku since both institutions had little international activities at the time. But Yamaichi had an extensive banking business abroad through subsidiaries. There was serious concern that its failure might trigger a crisis. Rather than declare "bankruptcy rehabilitation with protection from creditors," Yamaichi choose to "decertify" itself to avoid having its assets frozen. The Yamaichi failure prompted strong international pressure on Japan, especially from the United States, to increase the pace of dealing with the troubled financial system.

The failure of Hokkaido Takushoku and Yamaichi generated sharp declines in the stock prices of many financial institutions and a jump in the "Japan premium" in the international money market by around 100 basis points. The Japan premium is the additional basis points Japanese banks must pay for raising funds in overseas financial markets (figure 2.9). In response, the government proposed that it would provide a 30 trillion-yen fund, raised through bond issues, to assist bank recapitalization and consolidation as well as to protect depositors. This was a major departure from the past when the government had previously showed little willingness to use public funds to deal with financial problems. The government's previous position was not surprising, given the public outcry over its commitment of just 685 billion yen to

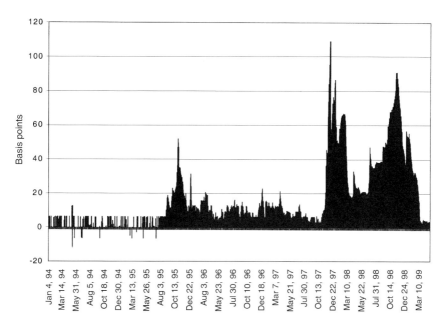

Figure 2.9
Japan Premium in the Eurodollar market: January 1994 to April 1999. The Japan premium is defined as the difference between the offshore interbank dollar rate in Tokyo, where most banks are Japanese and the interbank Euro dollar rate in the London, where most banks are western banks. In calculating the rates, the highest and lowest rates are dropped from sample. See Ito and Harada (2000) for details. Source: Ito and Harada (2000).

the housing loan company problem (*jusen*) in 1995 (Cargill, Hutchison, and Ito 1997). The much larger (30 trillion yen) commitment by the government met little opposition by the public or opposition parties this time, however, reflecting the concerns raised by the failures of such large and prominent financial institutions. These failures had apparently convinced the public that the problem was serious enough to justify a large-scale commitment of public funds to recapitalize the banking system and ward off the danger of a financial panic in Tokyo.

Of the 30 trillion yen, 13 trillion was set aside to compensate losses experienced by the deposit insurance system from failed institutions, while the remaining 17 trillion yen was designated for bank capital injections at the request of the bank. A special committee was set up to decide, upon request, which banks' would receive capital in the form of subordinated debts and preferred shares. The government used 1.8 trillion yen in March 1998 to purchase the preferred stock or subordinated debt of the 18 largest banks and three regional banks to help raise their capital ratios for the fiscal year ending March 31, 1998.

Confidence in the ability to handle the financial distress, however, was weakened when it was revealed the funds were more or less evenly distributed among the 21 institutions without any attempt at due diligence and no effort by the government to make a serious assessment of which institutions were viable without major restructuring. Confidence was further weakened by a series of financial scandals as it become increasingly evident the government had failed to disclose the extent of the problem. Police raids on the Ministry of Finance in early 1998 and suicides of several Ministry of Finance officials further weakened the credibility of Japan's most important financial regulatory authority. The Bank of Japan had until 1998 avoided scandal, though by the mid-1990s it had lost considerable public support for its role in the rise and fall of the bubble economy. However, improper conduct by officials of the Bank of Japan's Banking Bureau led to the arrest of one official and the resignation of the Bank's governor and deputy governor in early 1998. A Bank of Japan official in charge of internal management committed suicide in May 1998.

These events were followed by the resignation of Prime Minister Hashimoto in July 1998 as a response to the LDP's loss of the Upper House elections. This setback to the LDP was widely interpreted as a public rejection of the government's handling of the economic and financial problems. At the same time the financial and regulatory problems reached a crisis, the real sector problems intensified in late 1997 and brought Japan even closer to a panic situation.

2.6   Economic and Financial Distress Spreads

The economic and financial decline in Japan was the outcome of both failed policies to stimulate the economy and deal with nonperforming loans and insolvent financial institutions. External events also intensified Japan's economic and financial distress, raised world concern about contagion, and rekindled memories of the financial disruptions of the 1930s.

Financial crisis spread throughout the Asian region in mid-1997 as speculative attack, currency depreciation, and banking problems appeared first in Thailand and quickly spread to Indonesia and South Korea (Cargill 1998a). For the first time in the postwar period, the prospect of worldwide financial panic was seriously discussed in policy circles. Korea, while not as large or significant as Japan, was still the eleventh largest economy in the world. The financial distress in Korea and Japan together posed a serious threat to world stability.

Currency and equity markets in Europe and the United States felt the impact of the Asia crisis, and widespread concerns developed that a worldwide financial crisis could develop. The IMF (International Monetary Fund) provided $10 billion (of a total $40 billion package) to Indonesia, $3.9 billion ($17.2 billion total package) to Thailand and, in the largest commitment in IMF history, $21 billion to South Korea ($58 billion total package). The bailout was particularly difficult for Korea to accept because of its recent successes and status: three decades of 8 percent real GDP growth, OECD membership in 1995, and the perception that Korea would emerge as Asia's next economic giant.

In summer 1998 the Asian crisis appeared to spread further (Montes and Popov 1999). The Russian economy, which had exhibited serious economic, financial, and political problems since the early 1990s, collapsed under the weight of hyperinflation and declining growth. In August 1998 the Russian government devalued the ruble and defaulted on internal debt. This combined with the Asian problems adversely impacted financial markets throughout the world and had an especially negative effect on the ability of developing countries to raise funds and brought closer scrutiny to exchange rates and the ability of developing countries to service their external debt. By the end of the year, for example, Brazil had experienced a significant loss of reserves and required a 42 billion dollar program to resist currency depreciation. The program failed and, in January 1999, Brazil devalued its currency.

Japan's performance did not cause the Asian crisis nor contribute to the problems in Russia or Brazil in any meaningful sense. Japan had been experiencing economic and financial stress since 1990, and in most cases the problems in other countries in 1997 and 1998 could be attributed to factors other than Japan. Nonetheless, the spread of financial distress beyond Japan raised concerns about the stability of the international financial system. Also, because of Japan's importance, the Asian crisis brought more pressure on Japan, both internal and external, to take more aggressive action.

2.7 Is Japan's Banking Crisis Special?

In the 1980s and 1990s a number of industrialized countries experienced severe bank crises similar to that of Japan. Japan's experience seems to fit with the general characterization of the causes of banking crises in at least two ways: macroeconomic instability (boom and bust cycles in asset prices and real output) and weakness in financial structure (financial liberalization, deposit guarantees, and weak supervision and regulation).

An expansionary monetary and credit policy was clearly evident in Japan in the latter 1980s and contributed to the boom and bust cycle of asset prices. Equally important, financial liberalization was undertaken against the background of a weak financial structure—an increasing competitive financial environment, shifts in the flow of funds, inadequate supervisory oversight, incentives to take on increased risk, deficiencies in accounting and financial disclosure frameworks, and failure of government action to identify and manage the problem. Cargill (2000), Cargill, Hutchison, and Ito (1997, 1998), and Ito (2000) discuss these aspects of Japan's financial crisis in detail.

In some respects Japan's financial distress is thus similar to financial distress or banking problems experienced by a number of countries in the 1980s and 1990s. At the same time, however, the slow response of the regulatory authorities to resolve the problem and the subsequent long duration of the problem make Japan a special case among the industrial countries.

Identifying Bank Crises

In order to place the Japanese banking crisis in international context, Hutchison and McDill (1999a) considered the experiences of 20 industrial countries over the 1980 to 1997 period using annual data. The countries investigated are all OECD members: Australia, Austria, Belgium, Canada, Switzerland, Germany, Denmark, Finland, France, Great Britain, Greece, Ireland, Italy, Japan, the Netherlands, Norway, New Zealand, Portugal, Sweden, and the United States. They also looked at a broader group of countries with similar results (Hutchison and McDill 1999b). Using four bank crisis indicators (real GDP growth, exchange rate depreciation, credit growth, and stock market growth), seven countries are identified as having episodes of banking distress since 1980: Finland (1991–94), Italy (1990–94), Japan (1992–97), Norway (1987–93), Portugal (1986–89), Sweden (1990–93), and the United States (1984–91). Episodes of banking sector distress were identified and dated following the criteria of Demirguc-Knut and Detragiache (1998). A country was in a distress situation if (1), a large fraction of bank loans were nonperforming, (2), if a sizable government bailout using public

Table 2.2
Economic characteristics of industrial countries experiencing banking crises

	Countries not experiencing bank crisis	Countries experiencing bank crisis[a]	Difference in mean values: $Pr > \lvert t \rvert$	Japan
Real GDP growth	2.27	2.72	0.11	3.97
	(2.23)	(1.79)		(0.99)
Exchange rate	2.04	2.92	0.68	−5.41
depreciation	(13.00)	(15.08)		(13.64)
Inflation	5.57	8.66	0.00	2.12
	(5.39)	(6.18)		(1.22)
Real interest rate	3.33	1.91	0.00	2.55
	(3.65)	(3.12)		(0.89)
Credit growth	5.91	5.10	0.41	6.46
	(11.11)	(5.12)		(2.60)
Stock price change	11.62	23.16	0.01	13.90
	(19.30)	(29.50)		(18.60)
Budget surplus	−3.96	−5.12	0.12	−4.25
	(4.14)	(5.21)		(2.60)

a. Values prior to banking crisis.

funds occurred, (3), if widespread bankruptcies or forced mergers were evident, and (4), or if a run on bank deposit occurred.

Economic Characteristics

To what extent were the macroeconomic characteristics in Japan similar to those of other countries around the time of banking problems? Several basic macroeconomic characteristics are considered in tables 2.2 and 2.3. The variables considered are real GDP growth, the change in the spot exchange rate against the U.S. dollar (domestic currency price of the U.S. dollar), the rate of inflation, and the real interest rate. To investigate whether excessive money and credit growth and asset price bubbles are associated with banking distress, the rate of credit growth (credit) and the rate of change in stock prices (stock) were included as explanatory factors.

Table 2.2 shows the differences in these economic characteristics between the group of countries experiencing banking distress and the group that avoided serious banking problems. The average values of these indicator variables are calculated over the full sample period for those countries that have not experienced an episode of banking dis-

Table 2.3
Economic development before, during, and after bank crises

	Seven crisis countries				Japan		
	Prior to crisis	First year of crisis	During crisis	After crisis	1980 1991–	1992	1993– 1997
Real GDP growth: $Pr > |t|$	2.72 (1.79)	1.32 (4.19) [0.42]	1.47 (2.20) [0.93]	3.53 (1.46) [0.00]	3.97	1.02	1.45
Exchange rate depreciation	2.92 (15.08)	−4.68 (9.83) [0.10]	3.56 (10.73) [0.08]	−1.69 (8.21) [0.06]	−5.41	−0.36	0.82
Inflation	8.66 (6.18)	9.71 (12.8) [0.84]	4.09 (3.37) [0.29]	4.13 (3.94) [0.97]	2.12	1.73	0.06
Real interest rate	1.91 (3.12)	0.80 (10.26) [0.78]	3.73 (2.75) [0.48]	4.09 (3.93) [0.74]	2.55	1.52	1.07
Credit growth	5.10 (5.13)	2.77 (10.86) [0.59]	−1.078 (5.34) [0.39]	2.97 (4.61) [0.01]	6.46	1.17	0.83
Stock price change	23.16 (29.50)	−6.21 (18.57) [0.01]	11.21 (22.95) [0.01]	10.15 (14.32) [0.85]	13.90	−25.95	0.99
Budget surplus	−5.12 (5.21)	−4.59 (5.21) [0.81]	−5.62 (4.52) [0.65]	−4.75 (3.04) [0.49]	−4.25	0.31	−1.54

Note: Parentheses indicate the standard deviation of the variable. Brackets indicate the probability that the mean is different from the mean of the category to its left.

tress, and the average values of these variables are calculated over the period leading up to the banking problem in the focus group (banking distress group) of countries. The objective is to identify different movements in these variables that distinguish the banking distress and non-distress countries during the periods of relative tranquillity, namely before banking problems become critical.

The first column of statistics show the mean values for the countries not experiencing a serious banking problem, and the second column shows the mean values for the bank distress countries. The third column shows the mean difference (*t*-statistic) tests, and the fourth column presents the corresponding value for Japan over the period prior to the banking crisis. The standard deviations are shown in parentheses below the mean values.

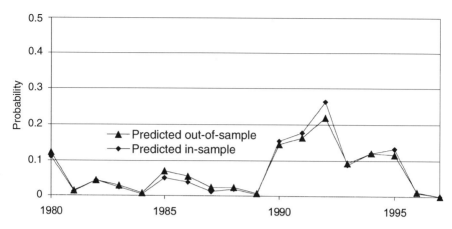

Figure 2.10
Predicted probability of a banking crisis in Japan.

The mean difference tests indicate that only the average rate of inflation and increase in stock prices are significantly higher in countries struck by severe banking problems. Average real GDP growth and average budget deficits also appear marginally higher (statistically significant at the 11 and 12 percent level, respectively) in the distress group. By contrast, the average level of real interest rates (short term) are lower in industrial countries experiencing banking problems—at least in the period prior to the crisis—than in the industrial countries not experiencing a serious episode of banking distress.

Where does Japan fit in this general pattern distinguishing economic developments in the banking distress countries from the non-distress countries? Similar to other bank-distress countries, Japan's average real GDP growth and rise in stock prices was faster than the group of industrial countries not experiencing severe financial problems. Prior to the start of the crisis, however, Japan experienced less exchange rate depreciation (indeed, strong appreciation), lower inflation, and somewhat higher real interest rates than either the other banking distress or the non-distress countries.

These variables along with other country-specific indicators such as central bank independence and labor unrest were used to estimate a probit model to predict episodes of banking distress.[1] Figure 2.10 reports the predicted probability of banking distress occurring in Japan during the 1980 to 1997 period. The line labeled "predicted in-sample"

---

1. See Hutchison and McDill (1999a, 1999b) for details.

uses the coefficient estimates from the probit model to predict the probability of a banking problem arising in Japan for each year. The probability was below 10 percent until 1990, at which time the probability jumps to over 15 percent. The probability climbs further to almost 20 percent in 1991 and peaks at about 30 percent in 1992. The estimated probability then drops sharply to below 10 percent in 1993. The Japanese financial system appeared to be particularly "vulnerable" or exposed to banking sector risk in the early 1990s.

Financial distress in Japan thus appears to be most closely associated with the rise and collapse of the bubble economy of the second half of the 1980s and early 1990s. Combined with the existing structure of the financial system, the collapse of asset prices is the key factor in explaining Japan's financial problems. In this respect the onset of Japan's banking crisis is comparable to similar banking problems in other countries. However, the relationship between financial distress and the decline in stock prices was especially strong in Japan due to a special feature of capital-asset requirements in Japan.

Structural Characteristics

Japanese banks commonly hold equities of their large corporate customers with which they have long-term relationships. These equities have typically been held for a considerable period of time, and as such, contain unrealized capital gains that are not reported on the balance sheet. Latent capital gains (difference between the current market value of the equities and their book value), sometimes referred to as "hidden" capital gains, have been a large buffer in the capital position among Japanese banks that have been undercapitalized.

In 1988, at the time of the adoption of the Basle capital-adequacy requirements, the Japanese regulatory authorities negotiated successfully for latent capital gains to be counted as part of near-capital or tier II capital. This was expected to make it easier for Japanese banks to meet the Basle requirements and looked reasonable in 1988 and 1989, before the asset-bubble burst. The counting of latent capital gains as part of bank capital combined with expansionary monetary policy, however, further fueled asset inflation as banks were able to increase lending at the same time equity price increases were increasing capital. The collapse of equity prices after 1990, led to a shortage of capital as latent capital gains fell significantly. What appeared to be a political success in 1988 quickly turned into a serious constraint on dealing with

Japan's banking problems as all of the major banks in Japan are subject to the Basle requirements.

2.8   The Japanese Economy in Comparative Perspective

Table 2.3 shows the economic characteristics of the industrial countries experiencing episodes of banking distress at different periods: prior to banking distress, the first year of the onset of the episode, during the bank problem, and after the episode. The number in parenthesis below the mean value is the standard deviation of the variable and the number in brackets is the probability that the mean value indicated is the same as the previous value. For example, real GDP growth after episodes of banking sector distress were resolved averaged 3.53 percent per annum (standard deviation of 1.46), a significant jump (less than 1 percent probability that the values are the same) from the 1.47 percent average (2.20 standard deviation) recorded during the distress episodes.

The "asymmetric" information explanation for bank crises, expressed for example by Kaminsky and Reinhart (1996), would suggest that a booming economy and sanguine views of the future (e.g., strong stock markets and rapid credit growth) would tend to be followed by a slowdown in economic activity and fall in stock values and credit growth. The basic time-series statistics support the "asymmetric view." The four variables which indicate a distinct shift over distress episodes are real GDP growth, exchange rate depreciation, credit growth and stock price rises. Real GDP growth drops during the episode of banking distress and rises significantly following the episode. Credit decreases during the bank problem and jumps markedly following the episode.

Perhaps the most striking feature is the development of stock markets: booming prior to an episode of distress (23 percent annual rise), sharply declining in the first year of the problem (average 6 percent drop), and rising around 10 to 11 percent per annum on average during the remaining years of the banking sector distress episode as well as following the episode. The 11 percent per annum stock price rise is the same as the average for the non-crisis countries over the full 1980 to 1997 sample period. Although not statistically significant, inflation and real interest rates also tend to decline after the onset of banking sector distress.

Japan experienced a similar pattern over time to other countries experiencing banking problems: a booming economy (rapid real GDP and credit growth and rising inflation) and strong asset markets (rapid stock price increase) prior to the bank crisis, followed by a sharp slowdown and falling asset prices. All of these indicators suggest that recession conditions and asset price deflation typically characterize banking crises and Japan clearly fits with this pattern.

Two distinctive features of the Japanese banking crisis stand out, however. First, the Japanese banking problem continued longer than the episodes of distress experienced by other industrial countries in similar circumstances. Rather than improve, Japan's banking problem grew from the first signs of distress in the early 1990s until reaching a critical point in late 1997. Moreover the problem remained acute in 1998 and 1999. Second, it is apparent from table 2.3 that the economic recovery following the first year of an episode of banking sector distress was robust for most industrial countries (average 3.5 percent real GDP growth). Japan, by contrast, languished; real GDP grew by only 1.5 percent annually from 1993 to 1997, declined by 2.5 percent in 1998, and virtually stagnated in 1999. Japan's economic performance of the 1990s is weak by comparison both with other industrial countries experiencing episodes of banking sector distress (at various points in time) and with other industrial countries during this same period.

In sum, the circumstances leading up to the Japanese banking crisis do not appear unusual by international comparison with other industrial economies over the past twenty-five years. But the duration of the episode and its cost, in terms of lost output (especially relative to potential output growth), are extraordinary. Cargill, Hutchison, and Ito (1997) argue that the slow and tentative response of the supervisory and regulatory authorities in Japan greatly contributed to the banking problem and its real cost to the economy. Hutchison and McDill (1999b) document these costs in an international comparative study and also argue that the slow policy response to resolve the Japanese banking crisis—partly due to bureaucratic inertia and partly to a political impasse and lack of public support—greatly contributed to its duration and ultimate cost.

As discussed above, however, structural factors also played a role in determining the timing, duration, and costs of the Japanese banking crisis by international comparison. Financial intermediation in Japan underwent a significant transformation from the traditional bank-dominated system to one characterized by open and competitive financial markets. A contraction in the size of the banking sector, and a reduction in the number of banks, would most likely have occurred even in the absence of the asset price collapse and serious nonperforming loan problem. Indeed, this process put substantial competitive pressure on banks as they sought out new forms of business both domestically and overseas. Further development in this direction appears inevitable, leading some analysts to predict a further substantial contraction in the Japanese banking sector over the next decade (Hoshi and Kashyap 2000).

2.9   Concluding Comments

Economic and financial distress characterized Japan's economy in the 1990s. The problem remained despite a number of attempts to stimulate the economy with monetary and fiscal policy, and to deal with nonperforming loans and insolvency of financial institutions with new measures to tighten financial supervision and regulation. Japan's financial stress in terms of banking problems can be explained in general by a set of factors that appear to account for banking problems in other industrialized economies.

The differences, however, are striking. Aside from being the second largest economy in the world with important real and financial linkages to many countries, Japan's economic and financial distress lasted almost a decade. A number of significant policy and institutional changes, introduced in the latter part of the 1990s, are the subject of the next three chapters.

Chapter 3 explores the evolution of the new financial supervision and regulatory framework and suggests the new framework has the potential to solve the nonperforming loan problem, impose greater discipline on financial institutions, and ensure that any future financial distress does not advance to the crisis stage as it did in late 1997. The focus of this new approach involves both institutional and attitudinal changes that sharply separate the new from the old financial supervision and regulation framework.

Chapter 4 discusses the significant changes in the institutional structure of the Bank of Japan that became effective April 1, 1998, while chapter 5 places these changes in international perspective. Institutional redesign of the Bank of Japan is intended to provide the Bank of Japan with greater flexibility to conduct monetary policy and perhaps make it less susceptible to the pressures that led it to expand the money supply in the late 1980s, and thereby contribute to the asset inflation.

3

The New Financial Supervision and Regulatory Framework

3.1 Introduction

Financial supervision and regulation have grown in importance during the past two decades as financial systems became more competitive and internationalized. Monetary authorities increasingly find themselves faced with the choice between allowing a bank to fail in an environment that requires penalties for poor portfolio decisions or to support a troubled bank for fear that a bank failure will aggravate systemic risk. The choice is even more difficult with the advent of financial distress that characterized the banking systems of many countries in the late 1980s and early 1990s (*Economist* 1997; Lindgren, Garcia, and Saal 1996).

Liberalization and financial distress have elevated the importance of financial supervision and regulation and have generated pressure for institutional change in the supervisory and regulatory framework. In the past, a variety of institutional structures were used to implement financial regulation and monetary policy. In some countries the central bank was deeply involved in financial supervision and regulation, while in others separate agencies such as the finance ministry were responsible.

Japan is no exception. Liberalization and financial distress elevated the importance of supervision and regulation. The Bank of Japan and the Ministry of Finance have been forced to consider bank failures in the conduct of monetary policy and the extent to which lender of last resort powers should be used to support individual institutions. Likewise Japan has had to reevaluate its regulatory institutions and, in 1997, established a new comprehensive regulatory agency—the Financial Supervisory Agency—to separate supervisory and regulatory power from the Ministry of Finance. In October 1998 the Financial

Reconstruction Commission was established as a high level independent agency operating directly from the Office of the Prime Minister.
The Commission is responsible for the resolution of troubled financial
institutions, financial crisis management, has the authority to inspect
and supervise financial institutions, and oversees the operations of the
Financial Supervisory Agency (Nakaso 1999).

The two new regulatory institutions have significantly reduced the
role of the Ministry of Finance in financial regulation and supervision.
Further change in the role and importance of the Ministry of Finance is
scheduled to take place in the next few years with planned administrative changes in the central government. Prime Minister Obuchi in
1999 secured legislation to reorganize and consolidate the central government (Choy 1999). The Japanese name of the Ministry of Finance,
Okurasho, will be changed to *Zaimusho* to more accurately reflect its
more limited role. It is likely the English name will remain, however.
Still, even without further change in the Ministry of Finance, the role
of the Ministry at the start of the next century will be considerably
reduced from what it was during most of the postwar period.

These changes in the institutions of financial regulation and supervision have two implications for the Bank of Japan. The reduced role and
power of the Ministry of Finance combined with the increased legal
independence of the Bank of Japan from the Ministry have provided
the Bank of Japan an unprecedented opportunity to develop an independent monetary policy. The institutional changes also have implications for the Bank of Japan's current role in bank supervision. The Bank
of Japan has traditionally been responsible for shared bank supervision with the Ministry of Finance through its Examination Bureau. The
Ministry of Finance is no longer responsible for bank supervision as
that has been transferred to the Financial Supervisory Agency. The
Bank of Japan, however, continues to supervise banks, and in fact this
responsibility was formalized in the new Bank of Japan Law. Still the
Financial Supervisory Agency and the Financial Reconstruction Commission may question whether the Bank of Japan should retain its
supervisory responsibilities.

This chapter focuses on the newly emerging financial supervision
and regulatory framework in Japan. While it may be somewhat pre-
mature to refer to the changing institutional design of financial supervision and regulation as fundamentally different than the previous
framework, sufficient change has occurred in the past decade to rea-

sonably differentiate between the "old" and the "new" supervision and regulation framework. The new framework contains many new elements that would likely mitigate the types of forces that were responsible for financial distress in the 1990s, and introduces policies needed to restore the health of Japan's financial system.

The end of the old framework and the emergence of the new framework occurred in a series of well-defined steps from 1991 through 1999. Before discussing these stages, however, the old framework is outlined to provided a basis for comparison with the new framework and to highlight the significant changes that need to occur to restore Japan's financial system and fulfill the objectives of the Big Bang proposals of November 1996. The transition is identified by six stages starting from 1991 through 1999. Each stage is identified in table 3.1 by selected events to differentiate one stage from the other. The new financial supervision and regulatory institutions emerging form the transition process are then discussed. The chapter ends with a general discussion of the role of central banks in financial supervision and regulation and implications for the Bank of Japan.

3.2   The Old System of Financial Supervision and Regulation

The financial system that emerged after the end of the war was rigidly regulated and administered. The regime can usefully be summarized by characteristics that differentiated Japan's financial regime (Aoki and Patrick 1994; Cargill 1998b; Cole 1993) from financial regimes of other industrial countries. The Japanese regime served as a model for developing Asian countries (Lee 1992) and thus played an important role outside of Japan.

Financial institutions were segmented in terms of sources and uses of funds, interest rates were regulated, and implicit and explicit credit allocation controls were pervasive. Market forces were not absent, but regulatory and administrative directions were more important than market forces in the flow of funds. Banks established long-term relationships with their borrowers in which the relationship, in some cases, assumed greater importance than objective evaluation and monitoring of credit risk.

The regime incorporated an official policy of no failures of financial institutions or markets. The no-failure policy was supported by extensive government deposit guarantees, limited portfolio flexibility of

Table 3.1
Transition from the old to the new financial supervision and regulation framework in Japan, 1991 to 1999

		Example
Stage I: 1991 to 1994		
Denial and forbearance	The existence of problems denied. All resolutions were postponed.	Small credit unions or cooperatives fail but are resolved within the existing framework of the Deposit Insurance Corporation. Losses are less than payoff equivalent, but no meaningful penalties are imposed, thus enhancing moral hazard.
	Stock prices decline causing latent capital to fall and decreases tier II capital.	First *jusen* resolution plan is proposed based on the hope of equity and land price recovery. Resolution plan is thus based on forbearance and forgiveness.
	The Ministry of Finance allows banks to issue subordinated debt purchased by life insurance companies. This is not a fundamental solution to capital shortage; it transfers bank risk to the insurance industry.	Ministry of Finance becomes aware of insolvent credit cooperatives but fails to take action.
		Several banks attempt to deal with nonbank subsidiary (leasing companies) problems, but other banks refuse to participate.
		Ministry of Finance takes no action despite being made aware of the problem of bank subsidiaries. It postpones the resolution of the leasing company problem.
Stage II: 1995 to 1996		
Financial distress recognized, but minimal policy response	The nonperforming loan problem increases. Small credit cooperatives fail, and in 1995 the first bank listed on the Tokyo Stock Exchange fails (Hyogo Bank). Strong intervention is required, but not forthcoming.	Turning point: Two credit unions fail (revealed December 1994, and a resolution scheme is announced in February 1995), and it becomes apparent that the Deposit Insurance Corporation cannot handle any more failures within existing framework.

Policy response retains elements of the old financial supervision and regulation framework	Deposit Insurance reserves are insufficient to entice the "white knight" institutions to bail out failed institutions.	Deposit Insurance Corporation recognizes its existing framework (payoff equivalent) is insufficient.
	A plan is needed to fill the funding deficiency.	Deposit Insurance Corporation forced to ask "related financial institutions" to contribute to resolving the two credit cooperative failures. Bank of Japan funds become part of the resolution as the Bank subscribes to shares of the Tokyo Kyodo Bank, the "white knight" that assumed the assets of the failed institutions.
	Jusen resolution (1996) helps protect agricultural cooperatives from losses but shifts losses to banks that founded the *jusen*.	
	Burden sharing represents a continuation of the convoy system. Banks are uncertain of their liability in the burden sharing. The market reacts by increasing the "Japan premium" in summer 1995.	Related financial institutions were requested to rescue failed institutions in the following cases: Cosmo Credit Cooperative (July 1995), Kuzu Credit Cooperative (August 1995), and Hyogo Bank (August 1995).
	Authorities and the Deposit Insurance Corporation are not empowered to issue cease and desist orders to financial institutions.	Hyogo Bank was the first bank listed on the Tokyo Stock Exchange to fail.
	Daiwa incident (August to October 1995) reveals the continuation of a policy nontransparency.	
	The Deposit Insurance Corporation is reformed and reorganized. Prompt Corrective Action adopted as part of overall deposit insurance reform. Complete government deposit guarantee announced to be in effect until March 2001	

Stage III: November 1996 to October 1997

Financial distress considered under control, institutional change, and the Big Bang announcement	The Big Bang.	Policy actions in 1996 combined with evidence of an economic recovery suggested financial distress can be reduced without additional policies.
		Big Bang plan announced.
		Big Bang is as much a political as an economic plan, but it reflects the continued influence of the old financial regime.

Table 3.1 (continued)

		Significant legislative changes followed the November 1996 Big Bang announcement, including exchange market liberalization, a "new" Bank of Japan, and a new super regulatory agency, the Financial Supervisory Agency.
		The Ministry losses power and influence as a financial regulatory authority and overseer of the Bank of Japan.

Stage IV: November 1997 to March 1998

Large-scale financial crisis and recession	30 trillion yen capital injection fund to protect depositors and resolve bank failures is proposed by the Miyazawa study group in December 1997 and passed by the Diet in February 1998.	Significant turning point occurs in the seriousness of the financial distress, marking the beginning of the end of the old financial framework.
	More transparent reporting of nonperforming loans by Ministry of Finance and Financial Supervisory Agency.	Hokkaido Takushoku fails in November 1997. This is the first city bank to fail. No immediate merger is in sight, so the decision is made to close the bank and liquidate its assets.
		Yamaichi, one of the Big Four securities companies, fails in November 1997.
		21 banks receive a total capital injection of 1.8 trillion yen March 1998; however, too little, too late, and no sanctions or meaningful conditions imposed on the 21 banks. Neither the financial position of the banks nor the market's perception of the financial distress changes. The "Japan premium" increases significantly after November 1997 and remains positive during 1998.

Stage V: April 1998 to February 1999

Continuation of economic and financial distress and recognition of the need to adopt new policies	Financial distress is finally recognized as far more serious than originally thought.	This is a significant turning point.
	Past policies of forgiveness and forbearance are recognized as failures.	The Financial Reconstruction Commission is established to provide more direct control over managing the financial crisis.

		Sizable public funding is invoked to resolve problems.	Long-Term Credit Bank and Nippon Credit Bank fail.
		60 trillion yen bonds are committed to raise funds to deal with financial distress.	Legislation to allow temporary nationalization and establishment of bridge banks to assume operations of failed institutions.
			Long-Term Credit Bank is temporarily nationalized, and the March 1998 capital injection is exposed as a failure.

Stage VI: March 1999 to end of 1999

March 1999 capital fund injection and shift to new regime	Government takes a more aggressive approach to resolving financial distress.	The temporarily nationalization of the Nippon Credit Bank reveals that the April 1997 capital injection and restructuring of Nippon Credit Bank were failed policies. The capital injection, involving the use of Bank of Japan funds, is a waste of public funding.
	Higher standards set for securing public funding than in March 1998.	A second capital injection is planned for March 1999.
		The 7.5 trillion additional yen injected in March 1999 is almost four times the amount of March 1998.
		Financial Reconstruction Commission imposes constraints on 15 banks receiving funds. Banks must present detailed restructuring plans, obtain additional capital in the private market, and allow close monitoring by the Commission, since most of the funding is in convertible preferred stock.
		Elements of the old regime that remain in place require a commitment from the banks to allocate lending to small- and medium-size businesses, to increase significantly government loan guarantees, and, from government banks, to increase their market share of lending.

individual institutions maintained by segmented markets, extensive restrictions on banking license and branch openings, and extensive administrative guidance by the regulatory authorities.

In the event an institution found itself in trouble, the Bank of Japan would provide funds or more likely, the Ministry of Finance would require stronger institutions to assist the weaker institution and in some cases, arrange a merger with a stronger institution. This system came to be referred to widely as the "convoy" system in which regulations were administered to support weak institutions (forgiveness and forbearance), and stronger institutions were required to support weaker and troubled institutions in the form of financial or merger assistance. The entire approach to dealing with troubled institutions was nontransparent. Nontransparency and lack of financial disclosure permitted the authorities to structure assistance programs without public comment and criticism and, at the same time, eliminate the potential for any loss of public confidence in the stability of the financial system.

This financial regime contributed importantly to Japan's emergence as the world's second largest economy by 1980; however, the success of the regime was based on a narrow set of circumstances that could not be sustained. Regulatory authorities were able to impose binding constraints on market forces by limiting the number of financial channels, segmenting financial institutions, and limiting financial disclosure. In addition the system required widespread consensus on a narrow set of industrial policies and high rates of economic growth to placate those excluded from the financial system and to support a policy of no failures of financial institutions and markets.

In the 1970s new economic, political, and technological forces emerged and changed the operating environment of Japan's financial regime. The narrow set of circumstances that had sustained the financial regime began to unravel. These new forces along with intense international pressure forced regulatory authorities to begin a process of financial liberalization in the late 1970s (Cargill and Royama 1988; Feldman 1986). Despite both the rhetoric of liberalization and implementation of a number of changes that relaxed constraints on the financial system, financial supervision and regulation remained wedded to nontransparency and an official policy that did not allow financial institutions to fail.

The old framework of supervision and regulation that formed part of this financial regime was prone to respond poorly to the type of stocks and financial distress that characterized Japan in the wake of the collapse of the bubble economy (Cargill 2000; Ito 2000). The framework's inherent emphasis on nontransparency ensured that the regulatory response would first be based on a policy of denial, followed by policies based on forgiveness and forbearance. Forgiveness and forbearance would be implemented by creative accounting approaches to understate the problem. Forgiveness and forbearance would ultimately fail as increased competition, both domestically and internationally, imposed penalties on all financial institutions, for example, the "Japan premium" which banks had to pay for funds raised in international markets. The failure of these policies would signal the end of the old supervisory and regulatory framework and the need to establish a new framework capable of dealing with financial distress consistent with open and competitive financial markets.

3.3 Transition from the Old to the New Financial Supervisory and Regulatory Framework

The collapse of the old and emergence of a new financial supervision and regulation framework occurred over six well-defined stages that followed the collapse of asset prices in the early 1990s. The following six stages may be identified in Japanese financial policy in the 1990s:

1. Denial and forbearance, 1991–1994

2. Financial distress recognized but minimal policy response, 1995–1996

3. Financial distress considered under control, institutional change, and Big Bang announcement, November 1996–October 1997

4. Large-scale financial crisis and recession, November 1997–March 1998

5. Continuation of economic and financial distress and recognition of the need to adopt new policies, April 1998–February, 1999

6. March 1999 capital injection and shift to new regime, March 1999–end of 1999

Table 3.1 outlines key elements of each of the six stages.

Stage 1: Denial and Forbearance (1991 to 1994)

The period from 1991 to 1994 is best characterized by denial that Japan faced serious financial distress and that the old financial framework

Table 3.2
Deposit Insurance Corporation assisted merger and loss-covers

			Deposit Insurance Corporation (unit = billion yen)			
Fiscal year[a]	Failed institu- tions[b]	Financial assistance, million yen[c]	Gross revenues	Expendi- tures	Net revenues	Reserves at the end of fiscal year
1992	2	20,000	94,411	20,169	74,241	770,626
1993	2	45,900	96,081	46,137	49,944	820,570
1994	2	42,500	98,140	42,680	55,459	876,030
1995	3	600,800	111,581	601,033	−489,452	386,578
1996	6	1,406,200	532,744	1,314,429	−781,685	−395,107
1997	7	390,600	464,318	163,229	301,089	−94,017
1998	30	5,363,700	1,675,820	2,769,430	−1,093,610	−1,187,628
1999	20	5,953,700				−1,749,500

a. Fiscal year from April 1 to March 31.
b. Dates of failures are those when the DIC executed the expenditure, and they are different from dates when failures were first announced.
c. Financial assistance is the sum of the monetary gift or inducement to the white knight institution and the purchase of assets before the failed institutions was merged with white knight institution. In addition to the above figures, 8 billion yen of subsidized lending to white knight institutions was made in 1992 and 4 billion yen of liabilities of failed institutions were assumed in 1997.

was no longer operable. Stock and land prices declined to less than half of their 1989–90 peak values. This put significant pressure on real estate and construction companies to service their debt and in turn deteriorated the balance sheets of the financial institutions that had lent to those industries. In October 1991 Toho Sogo Bank with 213 billion yen in assets was officially declared insolvent, though fraud played a role in this failure. Other institutions, however, were officially declared insolvent during the next few years (table 3.2) and their insolvency was a direct result of the collapse of asset prices.

The government responded to the financial problems with a series of disconnected actions that together delayed meaningful resolution of the growing nonperforming loan problem in the banking system. The actions were founded on the hope that stock and land prices would recover.

The series of unconnected actions failed to recognize the fundamental changes occurring in the financial system, enhanced moral hazard thereby increasing the ultimate resolution cost, and covered up the seriousness of the situation. These actions were predicated on the foundation of the old regime that the government had the ability to simultaneously manage market forces, maintain deposit guarantees, and support weak financial institutions until the expected recovery of the economy and asset prices. The policies amounted to nothing more than forgiveness and forbearance.

In 1992 the Ministry of Finance published nonperforming loan statistics only for the then 21 major banks combined and, reluctantly, in the following year published statistics for each of these banks. Regional banks only started to disclose nonperforming loans in 1994. The nonperforming loan statistics, however, were widely regarded as gross understatements because of the flexible definitions adopted by the Ministry of Finance and the reliance on bank self-reporting rather than independent audit verification. Nonperforming loans at that time were those loans where interest had not been paid in the past six months, while the U.S. standard classified loans as nonperforming if interest payments had not be made in the past three months. Restructured loans were defined as those with interest rates below the official discount rate at the time of the restructuring. Restructured loans with interest rates above or at the official discount rate were thus excluded in the definition of nonperforming loans.

The Ministry of Finance in 1992 permitted banks to issue subordinated debt to meet BIS capital-asset requirements since "latent" capital gains (unrealized gains on equities), which were counted as tier II capital, declined significantly with the collapse of asset prices. Life insurance companies purchased the subordinated debt and, according to many observers, were pressured by the Ministry of Finance to purchase the debt. This exposed the insurance industry to the risks in the banking industry.

The impact of declining land and housing prices on loan portfolios was especially severe for the *jusen* industry, which was represented by seven housing loan companies organized as bank subsidiaries (Cargill, Hutchinson, and Ito 1997). The insolvency of the *jusen* industry was known to the Ministry of Finance as early as 1992 and 1993, but was not revealed. Instead the Ministry of Finance adopted a rehabilitation plan in 1992 entirely based on the false assumption of recovery of land and housing prices.

In 1992 the Ministry of Finance encouraged the formation of the Cooperative Credit Purchasing Cooperation. The Cooperation represented the pooled funds of 162 banks intended to purchase nonperforming loans. The Cooperative Credit Purchasing Cooperation, however, essentially represented a warehouse, since few loans were actually sold, and as pointed out by Packer (2000), the real objective of the Cooperation was to provide significant tax advantages to those banks participating.

The Ministry of Finance encouraged a variety of "price-keeping operations" to raise equity prices. Administrative pressure was placed on a wide range on nonbank institutions to purchase equities and refrain from selling existing equity holdings. The Ministry of Posts and Telecommunications used postal life insurance funds to purchase equities.

Japan was forced to depart from its official policy of no failures of financial institutions or banks in 1991 when small credit cooperatives began to fail. Over the 1991 to 1994 period a total of six small credit cooperatives and banks were closed and their functions transferred to stronger institutions financed by funds provided by the Deposit Insurance Cooperation.[1] On the surface this policy appeared to be a sharp departure from the old regime; however, the approach to dealing with these small failed institutions revealed that little had changed. There was considerable evidence the Ministry of Finance was aware of the problems in these institutions for some time before any action was taken. Once action was taken, no penalties were imposed on uninsured depositors; employees of the failed institutions in most cases assumed new positions in the newly established institution, and no serious penalties were imposed on shareholders. The limited resources of the Deposit Insurance Corporation were thus wasted. The bailouts imposed no meaningful penalties and thus continued a modified version of the policy of no failures of financial institutions.

Thus, the policy actions by regulatory authorities, especially the Ministry of Finance, relied on an attitude that market forces could be managed and that nondisclosure or understatement provided time for weak financial institutions to improve their balance sheets once the anticipated recovery occurred.

Stage 2: Financial Distress Recognized but Minimal Policy Response (1995 and 1996)

The 1995 to 1996 period reflects a growing recognition of the financial distress and an effort to implement more focused policies. In December 1994 it became known that two credit cooperatives, Tokyo Kyowa Credit Cooperative and Anzen Credit Cooperatives, located in Tokyo

---

1. Cargill, Hutchison, and Ito (1996) and Milhaupt (1999) provide detailed discussion of deposit insurance in Japan.

collapsed. The resolution of the two failures (in 1995) required a creation of a "white knight" bank, Tokyo Kyodo Bank, which was funded partially by the Bank of Japan. The Tokyo Metropolitan Government was also asked to financially contribute to the resolution. These measures were necessary because the resolution costs exceeded the payoff equivalent amount that was a legal ceiling of the Deposit Insurance Corporation assistance. In fiscal year 1995 the Kizu Credit Cooperative collapsed, and its resolution exhausted the reserves of the Deposit Insurance Corporation.

The Ministry of Finance in late 1995 indicated that nonperforming loans as of September 1995 totaled 38 trillion yen, or about 4 percent of the loans held by depository institutions. While more realistic than estimates provided by the Ministry of Finance in the first stage, the official estimates grossly understated the magnitude of the problem. Cargill, Hutchison, and Ito (1997, p. 119), for example, raised the estimate of nonperforming loans to 46 trillion yen after making several adjustments. Some unofficial nonperforming loan estimates were twice as large as the official estimates.

In December 1995 the decision was made to reform deposit insurance and liquidate the insolvent *jusen* industry. To maintain public and international confidence in the financial system, the government announced in late 1995 a complete deposit guarantee until March 2001 and assured the public that financial distress was confined to the *jusen* industry and the smaller financial institutions. The government stated that it was not concerned about large institutions. The government's decision to guarantee all deposits was a reaction to an increasing fear among the public about the soundness of financial institutions.

These policies were based on a more realistic assessment of the degree of financial distress than in the first stage. Also the policies represented a more focused and connected set of policies. However, the government's response continued to rely on nontransparency, forgiveness, and forbearance. There was still a failure to recognize that the problems were a threat to the more central part of Japan's financial structure; that is, the large banks and securities companies.

Economic performance had not yet improved, worsening the banking problem and undermining the forebearance approach taken by the Ministry of Finance. Real GDP remained stagnant, equity prices failed to recover significantly, and land prices continued to decline.

The Ministry of Finance announced December 1995 that it intended to submit legislation to reform the Deposit Insurance Corporation and place it on a more sound foundation. The Deposit Insurance Corporation staff was expanded and moved from the Bank of Japan to a separate and larger location. The Deposit Insurance Corporation was also provided with more explicit rules for dealing with troubled financial institutions.

The Deposit Insurance Corporation was given the authority to assist mergers even if the amount of the funding exceeded the payoff equivalent to the failed institution, namely the DIC obligation for insured deposits or number of deposits times 10 million yen. The reserves of the Corporation were increased by raising insurance premiums from 0.012 percent of insured deposits to 0.084 percent of insured deposits plus a temporary increase of 0.036 percent. The higher premiums were used to fund two activities: to protect depositors up to the 10 million yen limit and to protect depositors above the limit of 10 million yen of failed cooperatives and other nonbank institutions. Variable insurance premiums were considered but rejected.

Deposit insurance reform was also accompanied by new policies for the Deposit Insurance Corporation to follow in dealing with troubled institutions. These formed the basis of a series of policies that were developed over the next year referred to as Prompt Corrective Action.

To assist in disposing of assets of troubled cooperatives, the government established the Resolution and Collection Bank to liquidate the assets of failed credit cooperatives. The Resolution and Collection Bank was originally Tokyo Kyodo Bank that had been previously established to resolve two credit cooperative failures.

The liquidation plan for the *jusen* industry involved establishing the Housing Loan Administration to dispose of assets of the jusen industry. Founding banks (parent banks) were required to relinquish all equity and loan claims to the *jusen*, and other banks were required to relinquish a little more than half of their claims. Agricultural cooperatives would be repaid all of their outstanding loans and would make a small "contribution" to the Housing Loan Administration of 530 million yen.

The relative magnitude of the burden share assumed by the credit cooperatives can be appreciated by comparing credit cooperative funds provided to the jusen industry as a percent of *jusen* assets in August 1995. Agricultural cooperatives provided 5.5 trillion yen of loans to support *jusen* assets of 13 trillion yen. Thus the 530 billion yen "contribution" represented a mere 10 percent of credit cooperative's exposure to the *jusen* industry. The sum of the contributions of the parent banks, other banks, and agricultural cooperatives fell short of the resolution cost by 685 billion yen which was provided by taxpayer funds.

These actions, while more focused than those pursued in the first stage, continued to retain key elements of the old framework. The Deposit Insurance Corporation reforms provided no independent authority to declare a financial institution insolvent. The development of Prompt Corrective Action policies as part of deposit insurance reform was not followed up with action to deal with larger institutions that were clearly market insolvent or close to market insolvent. The complete deposit guarantee announced by the government was more a stop-gap measure to calm depositors rather than part of a comprehensive framework to ensure stability while the government pursued an aggressive policy of Prompt Corrective Action. The Resolution and Collection Bank, like the Cooperative Credit Purchasing Cooperation, appeared to be another nonperforming loan warehouse.

The resolution of the *jusen* industry was fundamentally flawed and illustrated to the market the government's unwillingness to objectively assess and manage the financial crisis. It illustrated that the convoy system was still operational by imposing the greater part of the resolution burden on the banking system and essentially absolved the agricultural credit cooperatives of their role in financing the *jusen* industry. The intense public negative reaction to the small amount of taxpayer funding included in the plan gave the regulatory authorities the rationale to continue with a policy of forgiveness and forbearance. The negative public reaction was understandable given the nondisclosure policy practiced by the Ministry of Finance. As a result the government became very reluctant to propose the use of public funds to resolve the financial distress. This reluctance to use public funds further delayed resolution of the nonperforming loan problem and thereby substantially increased the ultimate resolution costs.

An incident occurred in summer 1995 regarding U.S. operations of Daiwa Bank that further revealed that the traditional thinking of Japan's supervisory authorities was still intact. In August 1995 huge losses resulting from the actions of one individual in the Daiwa's New York operation were revealed to the Ministry of Finance; however, the information was not reported to the Federal Reserve for six weeks. When the losses were finally revealed to U.S. regulatory authorities, Daiwa Bank's U.S. operations were suspended and purchased by Sumitomo Bank.

*Stage 3:   Financial Distress Considered under Control, Institutional
Change, and Big Bang Announcement (November 1996 to October
1997)*

The third stage starts with Hashimoto's Big Bang announcement of
November 1996 and the flurry of legislation that followed in the spring
and early summer of 1997. Policies during this stage appeared to be
following two distinct directions.

First, policies designed to deal with the financial distress manifested
by troubled financial institutions and nonperforming loans were not
aggressively pursued, although the importance of maintaining healthy
financial institutions was recognized. The government's complacency
was predicated on the significant policy actions taken in 1996 and
that economic recovery appeared to be taking hold, and hence would
reduce the size of the nonperforming loan problem.

Second, the Big Bang announcement represented a bold and an
accelerated approach to liberalization; however, the set of proposals
was not offered as a means of solving the current financial distress
but as a framework for Japan's financial system over the long run.
Financial distress was not ignored, but the improved economic performance and policy decisions made in 1996 with regard to deposit
insurance and the *jusen* industry rationalized the Big Bang's forward
perspective.

The Big Bang of Japanese financial markets was proposed in November 1996 by the Hashimoto government. Rather than a specific list of
policies, the Big Bang announcement emphasized the need for a new
financial structure by 2001 based on the following basic principles:

1. Free, open, and internationalized financial markets

2. Fair financial practices maintained by transparent and enforced
rules of conduct

3. Institutional changes (accounting, legal, and supervision) consistent
with international standards

The Big Bang was a bold and farreaching approach to restructure
Japan's financial services industry, but mainly it focused on future
directions and not on the financial distress experienced at the time of
its announcement. Rather than a set of specific policies, the Big Bang
introduced an attitude toward financial regulation and supervision
that in many ways was consistent with components of the regulatory
policies that had evolved in the United States during the 1980s and

1990s. Two perspectives help understand the Big Bang: the economic or policy content and the political economy of why the Big Bang emerged as a political platform.[2]

Economic and Policy Content

The policy content of the Big Bang would be defined by subsequent legislative and administrative changes carried out over the following few years. Despite the phrase "Big Bang," the announcement did not call for immediate and sudden change. The most important component of the Big Bang was a change in attitude about market forces, moral hazard, and transparency that, if implemented, would dramatically change the structure of Japanese finance from that which had dominated since 1950.

The first step was taken in April 1998 by deregulating the Foreign Exchange Law. Foreign exchange transactions were no longer restricted to being brokered by authorized banks. Japanese residents were permitted to directly open accounts in foreign institutions abroad. This immediately brought about greater competition from abroad. As a result domestic financial institutions (Japanese and foreign) became more aggressive in pursuing the large household saving estimated at 1,200 trillion yen. Foreign denominated money market mutual funds and foreign bonds became very popular since they offered higher yields than yen deposits and immediately increased competition. In fact the resulting capital outflow after the Foreign Exchange Law was liberalized is partly responsible for yen depreciation after April 1998.

The next steps were a series of legislative changes in the spring and early summer of 1997 that established the Financial Supervisory Agency and revised the Bank of Japan Law (Cargill, Hutchison, and Ito 1998). The new Bank of Japan Act and the Act establishing the Financial Supervisory Agency were submitted to the Diet in March 1997, and were passed by the summer. Both of these actions significantly altered the role of the Ministry of Finance in Japan's financial supervision and regulation framework; however, neither of the two new institutions would become effective until 1998.

The power of the Ministry of Finance to monitor and supervise the financial sector was transferred to the Financial Supervisory Agency. The Financial Supervisory Agency was to report directly to the Prime

---

2. Hoshi and Patrick (2000) provide several papers on the Big Bang proposal in the context of the financial problems in the late 1990s.

Minister, but this was modified in 1998 when the Financial Supervisory Agency was required to report to the Financial Reconstruction Committee established in October 1998. The Financial Supervisory Agency also was given responsibility to monitor and supervise agricultural cooperatives, labor cooperatives, and a wide range of finance and leasing companies. These institutions had been under the supervision of ministries other than the Ministry of Finance.

The 1942 Bank of Japan Law was revised to provide the Bank of Japan, one of the world's most formally dependent central banks, with enhanced formal independence from the Ministry of Finance. This legislation is discussed in chapter 4.

Japan's long-standing prohibition against the holding company structure of industrial organization would be removed. Government-funded corporations would be required to disclose financial information much like publicly traded counterparts.

In addition to these specific proposals and administrative policies, other rules and policies were introduced regarding accounting standards, reporting of nonperforming loans, and approaches to dealing with insolvent or close to insolvent financial institutions.

Political Economy
The rationale behind the policies endorsed by the Big Bang were well known, in some cases for decades. By the early 1990s the experiences of the United States and the Scandinavian countries with serious banking problems had clearly illustrated the need for a new regulatory viewpoint. The Big Bang was thus as much a political event as an economic event. The Liberal Democratic Party (LDP) had lost power in August 1993 when it lost its long-standing majority in the Lower House. It had previously lost its majority position in the Upper House in 1989; however, the Upper House is not the center of political power in Japan. The LDP regained the majority in the Lower House in 1996; however, this was accomplished only with coalition parties and a new platform.

The LDP after its 1993 loss was in search of a new political action platform. Structural reform had been on the agenda for many years, and despite some progress toward liberalization of Japan's markets, the process was far from complete. Frustration with the slow pace of reform, increasing magnitude of the nonperforming loan problem from 1993 to 1995, collapse of the *jusen* industry, and increasing foreign pressure to deal with the financial distress provided the LDP an opportunity to seize the agenda of the Big Bang as part of a new political reform. Two events rendered financial liberalization and reform a political winner.

First, the actions taken in 1996 with regard to deposit insurance and the *jusen* industry, combined with a fledging economic recovery in 1996, led many to believe that the nonperforming loan problem would soon be solved without aggressive policies toward large financial institutions. Thus the LDP could adopt a reform platform without having to make politically difficult decisions in dealing with the financial system and, especially, would not be required to ask for public funding. The foundation of the Big Bang, despite the vision of a radically different financial regime, was predicated on the belief that the past policy of forbearance and forgiveness had been successful and that economic recovery would solve the financial distress.

Second, the relationship between the LDP and the Ministry of Finance had deteriorated in the previous few years to the extent the LDP no longer owed an alliance to the Ministry and thus could adopt a plan opposed on many points by the Ministry. The long-established relationship between the LDP and the Ministry of Finance changed in 1993 when the LDP lost power. According to Mabuchi (1998), the Ministry of Finance had three choices at that time. The Ministry of Finance could continue to maintain the long-established alliance with the LDP, establish a relationship with the new parties in power, or remain politically neutral and wait for the return of the LDP.

The Ministry of Finance chose the second option of cooperating with the new administration and distancing itself from the LDP. Thus, when the LDP returned to power in 1996, the past relationship with the Ministry of Finance could not be reestablished on the same grounds. The LDP and Prime Minister Hashimoto were more willing to independently adopt a bold platform of reform that conflicted with the slow and projectionist policies of the Ministry of Finance. The LDP's position on this issue was strengthened by the loss of the Ministry's reputation. The Ministry of Finance's ability to counter the new platform was significantly reduced and, as a way to reestablish its reputation, the Ministry of Finance realized that support for the Big Bang proposals would be in its self-interest.

The Ministry of Finance thus became an advocate of the Big Bang. As will be discussed in chapter 4, this is the context needed to understand why the Ministry of Finance became an advocate of central bank reform in 1996. The Ministry's support of the Big Bang, including Bank of Japan independence, was viewed by the Ministry of Finance as a way to deflect criticism for past policy errors and to retain whatever regulatory and supervisory power was possible in the new and less friendly political environment.

Stage 4: Large-Scale Financial Crisis and Recession (November 1997 to March 1998)

The situation changed significantly in late 1997 as a result of external and internal shocks to the Japanese economy. Banking problems and general financial distress became a common feature of many Asian economies. Problems in Thailand, Malaysia, Indonesia, and other Asia economies emerged in summer and fall 1997, followed by financial distress in Hong Kong, albeit only briefly, and finally Korea in late 1997. The Korea situation was especially serious because, like Japan, it was a large economy playing an important role in the world trading system.

These external events had two effects on Japan. First, they heightened a general sense of international concern about the region and brought increased international pressure on Japan to more effectively deal with its six-year-long banking and nonperforming loan problem. Second, the general economic decline slowed Japan's economy and exposed Japanese financial institutions to further loan losses.

The most dramatic events in late 1997, however, were internal. The failures of Hokkaido Takushoku, one of Japan's city banks (largest twenty banks), and Yamaichi Securities Company, one of Japan's four largest security companies, in November 1997 were significant turning points in recognition of the pervasiveness and seriousness of the financial distress in Japan. The failure of a city bank, the first ever for Japan in the postwar period, and a large securities company were a shock and warning call that the financial distress could not be confined to small banks and credit cooperatives.

The market responded dramatically to the two failures and uncertainties about the government's resolve to deal with the financial distress. Bank stock prices declined relative to the market (figure 3.1) and the "Japan premium" increased 100 basis points on the international market (figure 2.9). The failures, especially Hokkaido Takushoku, represent a significant turning point in public confidence in the stability of the banking system.

Financial distress now extended to two large financial institutions and there was concern that other large financial institutions would fail. Confidence in the convoy system was completely shattered. The con-

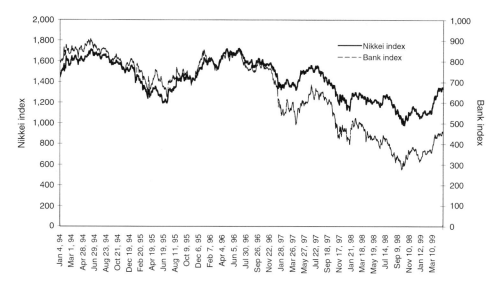

Figure 3.1
Nikkei 225 and Bank Stock Index: January 1994 to January 1999. Source: Ito and Harada (2000).

voy system was predicated on the existence of a large number of healthy institutions that could absorb losses of weaker institutions. The failure of Hokkaido Takushoku and Yamaichi Securities Company, however, suggested that even Japan's larger institutions were not above the problems permeating the system and that no large institution would be able to assist troubled institutions as had been the practice in the past. This was a sharp rejection of the government's promise in 1995 that no large financial institutions would fail[3] and raised concern over the credibility of the government's complete deposit guarantee announced in 1995.

The sense of financial crisis heightened in December 1997 despite the hint of a fiscal injection by the government in the near future. The call market dried up as many institutions became suspicious of the liquidity positions of other institutions. Lending and credit lines to small and medium-sized businesses were withdrawn. Some businesses complained that they were being squeezed for liquidity. As a result it became increasingly apparent to regulatory authorities that past policies had failed to deal with the financial distress that was now in its seventh year, and that a new supervisory and regulatory regime would

---

3. Some Ministry of Finance officials assert that the promise only pertained to large institutions, whose failure would have international spillover effects.

be needed. The sense of financial crisis was further heightened by evidence the hesitant recovery was being replaced with declining output and increasing unemployment, thereby increasing the size of the nonperforming loan problem.

In response and in an effort toward greater transparency, the Ministry of Finance officially acknowledged on January 12, 1998, what outsiders had been maintaining for years: The nonperforming loan problem was far larger than previous official estimates. The Ministry reported that at the end of September 1997, nonperforming loans totaled 76.7 trillion yen for all banks, excluding credit cooperatives, with revised loan categories. The new loan categories were based on possible risk assessment in addition to past overdue and bankrupt borrowers by individual banks. This classification scheme has become the standard for assessing the nonperforming loan problem in Japan.

Banks are required to classify their outstanding loans into one of four categories. Class I consists of loans with little or no risk of default. Class II consists of loans with some risk that requires monitoring. Class III consists of loans that are unlikely to be repaid, and class IV consists of loans that are unrecoverable. There was, however, a question as to whether internal estimates of problem loans under the new classification scheme would be accurate. The Financial Supervisory Agency found, for example, that internal self-reporting overstated class I loans and understated the three other classes in a survey of the top 19 banks for loan classifications for March 31, 1998.

In December 1997 the Miyazawa study group in the LDP recommended that 30 trillion yen needed to be raised to deal with the financial problem, protect depositors, and inject new capital into the banking system. Of the 30 trillion yen, 13 trillion were to be used to inject capital to solvent, but thinly capitalized banks, while the remaining 17 trillion were to be used to protect depositors of failed banks.

The Deposit Insurance Corporation in December 1997 was provided with additional powers. It was given the authority to arrange mergers between two troubled institutions instead of being confined to mergers between a troubled and healthy "white knight" institution. The Corporation in early 1998 was given the authority to issue its own bonds and special accounts were established to use public funds to purchase preferred stock and subordinated debt from financial institutions.

This stage was a significant policy turning point for two reasons. First, the government took a more aggressive approach to Hokkaido Takushoku. After several months of an unsuccessful effort to find a "white knight" bank, the Ministry of Finance allowed Hokkaido Takushoku to fail and proceeded with liquidation. Second, the 30 trillion yen bond issue represented a large commitment of resources and the end of the government's reluctance to use public funds. Political willingness to use public funds to recapitalize weak but viable banks would contribute to a faster resolution of the financial distress.

In order to prepare for the March 1998 capital injection, a special committee was formed under a law that was hastily passed and enacted on February 18, 1998. The Financial Crisis Management Examination Committee (chaired by Yoko Sazanami) met six times in February and March before authorizing a 1.8 trillion yen capital injection to 21 banks (9 city banks, 3 long-term credit banks, 6 trust banks, and 3 regional banks). Each bank was authorized to receive about 100 billion yen, irrespective of their relative financial condition. This was expected to raise the BIS risk-based capital ratio by less than one percentage point, except for the Long-Term Credit Bank and Nippon Credit Bank, which were expected to achieve a more than one percentage point increase in the capital ratio. The conditions for the capital injection were lax, however. No serious restructuring or aggressive write-down of nonperforming loans was planned. As a result the March 1998 capital injection was a failure, most clearly revealed when the Long-Term Credit Bank and Nippon Credit Bank both failed later in 1998.

The fourth stage started with external and internal shocks followed by policies that on paper appeared to be a significant shift from the old to a new financial supervision and regulation framework. The willingness to inject public money into the banking system was a major shift in policy during the crisis; however, it fell far short of its potential. When implemented, however, the policies were too little, too late, and continued to retain elements of the old financial supervision and regulation framework.

Stage 5: Continuation of Economic and Financial Distress and Recognition of the Need to Adopt New Policies (April 1998 to February 1999)

The March 1998 capital injection was widely criticized. The market's reaction was clearly negative as it had no effect on the downward trend in bank stock prices (figure 3.1) and no meaningful effect on the "Japan premium" (figure 2.9). In the opinion of many, it illustrated Japan's unwillingness to make the hard decisions to differentiate between institutions that had a meaningful chance of survival and those that for all practical purposes were already insolvent with no meaningful chance of becoming viable no matter how much capital was provided.

From the second to the fourth quarter of 1997 the economy had been stagnant with essentially zero growth; however, the financial distress was now accompanied by a serious economic downturn. Real GDP declined in the fourth quarter of 1997 and throughout 1998 (figure 2.1). The unemployment rate of 4.4 percent in November 1998 was higher than the unemployment rate in the United States.

Financial distress also increased. Nonperforming loans (class II + class III + class IV loans) at all banks (including the Long-Term Credit Bank and Nippon Credit Bank) were estimated at 73.1 trillion yen as of September 1998 (Table 3.3) representing 12 percent of outstanding loans or 10 percent of GDP. This estimate did not include non-performing loans already provisioned; for example, those banks that had previously failed, such as Hokkaido Takushoku, Tokuyo City, Kyoto Kyoei, Naniwa, Fukutoku, and Midori, but had not been merged or sold were not included in the estimates. Table 3.3. also indicates different concepts of nonperforming loans used in Japan.

Eight years of government and private-sector bank effort to resolve the nonperforming loan problem had not reduced the size of nonperforming loans nor did the unprecedented capital injection of March 1998 substantially strengthen the receiving financial institutions. The market punished banks and especially the weaker institutions, as bank shares were sold in the stock market. In mid-June, 1998, the stock price of the Long-Term Credit Bank plummeted and raised concern over its viability. An announced merger of the Sumitomo Trust Bank and the Long-Term Credit Bank on June 26, 1998, was received with skepticism. Estimation and separation of the nonperforming from the performing loans became a condition of the merger talks.

The Financial Supervisory Agency formally started business with some 400 staff members on June 22, 1998. Examining the financial condition of the major banks and in particular, the financial condition of the Long-Term Credit Bank, the Financial Supervisory Agency concluded that the Bank was seriously in trouble when it became apparent that some of its losses had been hidden in subsidiaries. The issue then became political as the opposition parties focused on the continuing financial crisis as evidence of the policy failures of the ruling parties. While discussion and negotiation continued through the summer, the balance sheet of the Long-Term Credit Bank deteriorated further.

Table 3.3
Nonperforming loans among all banks according to different classifications, September 1998 (unit = trillion yen)

		Conversion		
Loans to bankrupt borrowers	7.1	Fully provisioned (→Class I) Collateralized (→Class II) Not provisioned (→Class IV)	Class IV	0.1
Overdue loans	14.6	Fully provisioned (→Class I) Collateralized (→Class II) Not provisioned (→Class III)	Class III	6.9
Restructured loans	8.4	Class II	Class II	66.1
NPL subtotal	30.1			
Normal	515.4	Risky borrowers (→Class II) Others (→Class I)		
			II + III + IV subtotal	73.1
			Class I	525.0
Total loans	545.5		Total loans and credit	598.0

Note: Two different approaches to defining nonperforming loans:

Banking Association Disclosure Rule

1. Loans to bankrupt borrowers. Borrowers are legally bankrupt, so there is little chance that loans will be collected. Uncollected interest is not listed as a receivable.
2. Overdue Loans. Interest payments overdue more than three months. Until 1997 only loans with interest payments overdue more than six months category were available.
3. Restructured Loans. Loans that have been restructured with reduced interest rates, grace periods, debt reduction, and other considerations that favored the borrower.
4. Normal. All other loans.

This classification of nonperforming loans is based on the Bankers' Association Standard; therefore it is possible to make comparisons across banks. Individual banks are encouraged to disclose their nonperforming loans. The Ministry of Finance until June 1998, and Financial Supervisory Agency after July 1998, announce the aggregate data on nonperforming loans according to the Bankers' Association Standard.

Classified Loans

1. Class IV. It is impossible to collect the loan or credit. The loan or credit has no value.
2. Class III. There is serious doubt about loan and credit collections. Although it is highly possible that the full value of the loan or credit will not be collected, it is difficult to estimate how much can be recovered.
3. Class II. Not all the standards for credit-worthy borrowers are satisfied. Collection risk is above normal. The individual bank assesses the collection risk.
4. Class I. All other loans and credits.

This classification of nonperforming loans will not include all nonperforming loans defined by the Bankers' Associations rule. Fully provisioned or loans with collateral are classified as Class I or Class II loans. The classification (especially Class II) is subjective to individual banks, and not comparable across banks. The aggregate nonperforming loan estimates are disclosed by the Financial Supervisory Agency. The base includes credits as well as loans.

New laws focused on financial reconstruction and crisis management were passed in October 1998. They established the Financial Reconstruction Commission as part of the Prime Minister's Office to coordinate the management of the financial crisis, to supervise the Financial Supervisory Agency, and to strengthen deposit insurance. They established three schemes of dealing with failed financial institutions: a "temporarily nationalized bank" scheme, a "bridge bank" scheme, and a liquidation scheme.

The total fiscal underwriting for financial reconstruction was expanded to 60 trillion yen. The Long-Term Credit Bank applied for, and was accepted, as a temporarily nationalized bank on October 23, 1998. This was further evidence that the March 1998 capital injection was a failure because of an unwillingness and/or inability to distinguish between near-insolvent and more healthier banks that had a good chance of reestablishing viable operations. The essentially equal capital infusion for each bank ensured the money would be wasted on the near-insolvent banks while the capital injection for the healthier banks would be insufficient.

The framework set up by the October 1998 legislation and the decision to nationalize the Long-Term Credit Bank represented the first time, since the start of the financial distress in 1991, that the authorities seriously considered how to resolve large financial institution failures in an orderly and consistent manner. This indeed was a change in attitude, which would again be tested with Nippon Credit Bank. In December 1998 Nippon Credit Bank was determined to the insolvent and nationalized. In fact the Financial Supervisory Agency revealed that based on their examination, Nippon Credit Bank had been insolvent since the end of March 1998. Just as the failure of the Long-Term Credit Bank illustrated the policy errors of the March 1998 capital injection, the failure of Nippon Credit Bank illustrated the policy error of an April 1997 reform plan for Nippon Credit Bank organized by the Ministry of Finance and the Bank of Japan. As a result of the failure of Nippon Credit Bank, the Bank of Japan, as well as several private banks, lost the value of their subscriptions to Nippon Credit Bank shares that were part of the April 1997 reform plan.

The decisions and actions with regard to the Long-Term Credit Bank and Nippon Credit Bank elevated the reputation of the Financial Supervisory Agency and its head, Mr. Yanagisawa. They suggested that a new financial supervision and regulatory regime was indeed emerging in Japan and that the old system based on nontransparency and mutual support was no longer applicable.

In the wake of the financial crisis, regulatory authorities adopted a more liberal view to foreign capital and foreign institutions in dealing with the financial distress. Merrill Lynch was permitted to purchase Yamaichi Securities Company, instantly enlarging the presence of foreign financial institutions in Japan's domestic retail securities market. Outside auditors were frequently being used to provide credibility to assessing the financial condition of Japanese institutions (due diligence); for example, several months prior to the failure of Hokkaido Takushoku Bank, Sumitomo Trust Bank had utilized U.S. firms to conduct audits of Hokkaido's condition.

As part of the October 1998 legislation, the Resolution and Collection Organization was established to consolidate the activities of the Resolution and Collection Bank and the Housing Loan Administration. The latter two agencies were established in 1995 and 1996, respectively, to dispose of the assets of failed credit cooperatives and the *jusen* industry, respectively. The new organization was structured as a private corporation and used funds provided by the Deposit Insurance Corporation to purchase nonperforming loans from insolvent institutions, fund special bridge banks that were envisaged to assume the operations of failed institutions, and fund other institutions. The new agency was based on the U.S. Resolution Trust Corporation established in 1989 to liquidate the assets of insolvent savings and loan associations.

The government announced a more aggressive application of Prompt Corrective Action. There would be two sets of policies, depending on whether a bank was insolvent or merely weakened. Insolvent banks would be liquidated, placed on "special public control" (temporarily nationalized), or converted into a government-managed "bridge bank." In the case of weak, but solvent internationally active banks, the government could at the request of the bank, inject public funding by purchasing common stock, preferred stock, or subordinated debt. However, capital injection with common shares would only be available to "significantly" and "critically" undercapitalized banks, that is, banks with risk-adjusted capital of 4 to 2 percent and under 2 percent, respectively. Banks with ratios between 4 and 8 percent may receive capital injections with preferred shares or subordinated debt, while banks with adjusted capital ratios above 8 percent could receive capital injections with preferred shares or subordinated debt if they assisted in a merger or purchased a weaker institution or were regarded as systemically important by the government. The "trip-wire" capital asset ratios are one-half the level for internationally active banks.

Stage 6: March 1999 Capital Injection and Shift to New Regime (March 1999 to end of 1999)

The preceding stage was the most dramatic policy change of the entire decade of dealing with the financial distress and represented a meaningful turning point in the emergence of a new financial supervisory and regulatory regime. The stage started with a failed capital injection scheme tied to the old regime of mutual support and nontransparency. The stage ended with a serious effort to establish an infrastructure for the orderly resolution of bank failures and commitment of a total fund of 60 trillion yen to resolve the financial distress in the banking system. Although the October 1998 legislative changes were pushed and supported by the opposition parties, the Obuchi government finally provided the critical support to achieve the legislative changes. A second, but larger capital injection, based on the new approach was planned for March 1999.

The key element of the new approach would be how the committed funds would be used to resolve financial distress. To be credible, the March 1999 injection had to depart from the approach used in March 1998. The March 1998 injection was lax, nondiscrimentating, and showed an unwillingness of the government to depart from the old financial regime.

The March 1999 injection of public funds was based on the same framework as March 1998: banks had to request funding, requesting banks had to demonstrate positive net worth, and requesting banks had to demonstrate a plan that would permit them to remain viable in the long run. While the framework was similar, the implementation was significantly different. The Financial Reconstruction Commission, in charge of the capital injection, raised the standards for securing public funding. The definition of net worth was made more rigorous, higher standards were applied to classifying loans into class I, II, III, and IV categories, and banks were required to submit detailed and meaningful restructuring plans (International Monetary Fund 1999, Annex II). Restructuring plans had to include four elements: expansion of portfolio activities to sustain profits, cost reduction measures, strategic alliances with other institutions, and balance sheet adjustments directed at disposing of nonperforming loans and requiring banks to seek new capital from the private market.

Table 3.4 presents the distribution and terms of the public funding to the 15 banks that made an application for funds. The March 1999 injec-

Table 3.4
March 1999 injection of public funds

	Total funds	Convertible preferred shares		Non-convertible preferred shares	Subordinated debt	Percent average yield
		Amount	Grace period (months)			
City banks						
Dai-Ichi Kangyo	900	400	64	300	200	1.27
Fuji	1,000	500	66	300	200	1.05
Sakura	800	800	42	0	0	1.37
Sanwa	700	600	27	0	100	0.54
Sumitomo	501	501	37	0	0	0.71
Asahi	500	400	39	0	100	1.25
Daiwa	408	408	3	0	0	1.06
Tokai	600	600	39	0	0	0.95
Long-term credit bank						
Industrial Bank of Japan	600	350	51	0	250	1.06
Trust banks						
Mitsubishi Trust	300	200	52	0	100	1.34
Sumitomo Trust	200	100	24	0	100	1.28
Mitsui Trust	400	250	3	0	150	1.44
Chuo Trust	150	150	3	0	0	0.90
Toyo Trust	200	200	3	0	0	1.15
Regional bank						
Bank of Yokohama	200	100	28	0	100	1.50
Total	7,459	5,559	—	600	1,300	1.09

Source: Financial Reconstruction Commission, obtained from International Monetary Fund (1999).
Note: In billions of yen, unless otherwise specified.

tion totaled 7.5 trillion yen compared to 1.8 trillion yen in March 1998. The majority of injection to any one bank was in the form of convertible preferred shares with a "grace period" condition attached. The grace period is the period of time the government may convert the preferred shares into common stock. In the case of the weakest institutions (Dai-Ichi Kangyo, Fuji, etc.), the government has considerable influence over the operations of the bank for up to five years, converting its preferred to common stock and essentially nationalizing the bank. Stronger banks (Daiwa, Toyo Trust, etc.) have less restrictive conditions with grace periods of only a few months. The cost of the public funds was low and did not vary significantly from bank to bank, indicating the large subsidy element in the capital injection.

Table 3.5 presents elements of the bank restructuring plans submitted by the requesting banks. The most notable feature of table 3.5 is the planned reduction in staff. Each bank, over a four-year period, plans to significantly reduce staff and expenses. This is a major departure from Japan's traditional approach to employment. The dramatic cuts in employment planned by the banks, however, are consistent with restructuring in nonfinancial businesses. To illustrate, in late 1998 the former government owned telecommunications giant NTT announced plans to reduce employment by 20,000 by the year 2003, and Nissan Motor Co. made a similar announcement to cut some 20,000 jobs.

The market recognized the significance of the March 1999 capital injection and the new framework. The Japan premium disappeared in April 1999. The decisive actions of Financial Supervisory Agency along with the October 1998 legislative changes appear to have contributed to a recovery of confidence in Japan's financial institutions and markets.

The March 1999 capital injection was also accompanied by continued progress to implement the goals of the Big Bang. The fixed brokerage commission system long a part of Japan's equity markets was completely abolished October 1, 1999, for all transactions, completing a process started April 1998 when the fixed system was abolished on trades of 50 million yen or more. Access to the securities industry was simplified and the established exchanges' monopoly on stock trade was abolished so that equity trade could take place outside of the established exchanges. The financial services industry appeared ready to undergo an "Internet" revolution.

Consolidation was occurring rapidly in the financial services industry. In the past consolidation was encouraged by the government as

Table 3.5
Restructuring plans of major banks receiving March 1999 injections, FY 1998 to FY2002 (percent change over period)

	Net income	Gross income	Operating expenses	Personnel costs	Number of employees	Number of directors	Number of branches Domestic	Overseas
City banks								
Dai-Ichi Kangyo	19.8	3.0	−7.8	−16.1	−18.2	0.0	−13.2	−20.5
Fuji	50.9	18.7	−8.0	−10.1	−8.8	−17.1	−7.7	−15.2
Sakura	35.3	8.2	−10.2	−16.4	−21.0	−58.8	−24.9	−29.6
Sanwa	13.7	6.3	−2.3	−15.4	−16.2	−62.5	−7.5	−7.5
Sumitomo	6.6	−1.6	−9.0	−5.6	−13.3	−11.6	−6.7	−23.4
Asahi	14.8	8.6	−6.9	−5.9	−7.8	−10.3	−2.1	−68.4
Daiwa	25.1	0.1	−15.3	−17.0	−17.5	−35.5	−11.8	−100.0
Tokai	20.2	2.8	−10.6	−16.9	−12.5	13.3	−10.0	−48.8
Long-term credit bank								
Industrial Bank of Japan	−11.9	−12.6	−9.9	−0.9	−6.2	−42.9	−11.1	−22.2
Trust banks								
Mitsubishi Trust	−53.3	−28.1	−0.6	−7.1	−2.8	−13.9	−9.4	−47.4
Sumitomo Trust	−14.6	−1.6	−2.9	−14.8	−11.9	−9.4	−3.6	−53.8
Mitsui and Chuo Trusts	17.0	23.8	−6.3	−1.8	−10.8	−20.0	−12.7	−70.0
Toyo Trust	39.0	10.3	−14.3	−17.2	−14.6	−40.0	−35.7	−80.0
Regional bank								
Bank of Yokohama	—	—	—	−14.9	−21.1	−36.8	—	—
Total	11.5	3.4	−7.9	−11.6	−13.8	−26.5	−11.7	−31.4

Sources: International Monetary Fund (1999), Merrill Lynch, and *Nikkei Weekly*.

a method for dealing with financial distress; however, in 1999 there appeared to be less pressure by the government to force white knight acquisitions. The reduced pressure was the outcome of new policies to deal with troubled institutions and the continued elimination of financial institutions through failure. Consolidation in 1999 became more of a market-driven force as various institutions found that mergers, acquisitions, and restructuring would place them in the best position to compete in the new and more open competitive environment (*Wall Street Journal*, January 21 and February 8, 1999). The most dramatic example of this occurred August 1999 when Dai-Ichi Kangyo Bank, Fuji Bank, and the Industrial Bank of Japan announced plans to merge. When completed (planned for April 2001), the new institution will be the largest bank in the world.

In sum, the events of March 1999 and through the remainder of the year suggested that a meaningful turning point had been reached. The March 1999 injection was a meaningful departure from March 1998, and continued liberalization of equity markets, bank restructuring, government induced consolidation, and market induced consolidation of financial institutions were impressive. At the same time, one could identify a number of new problems embedded in some of the policies and the continuation of old problems that cast a shadow over efforts to establish a new financial regulation and supervision regime.

First, banks receiving public funding were required to devote part of their lending to small and medium sized business; second, government loan guarantees were significantly expanded; and third, lending by government banks for small business and housing increased (Cargill and Yoshino, 2000). The credit allocation policies and enhanced government involvement in the flow of funds were troublesome. The policies, although well intended from a macroeconomic point of view, were likely to continue, since they would establish a political base that will make it difficult to reverse the polities as Japan's economy and financial position improve.

A number of old problems remained. Nonperforming loans remained large, and little effort was made to dispose of the assets. Nonperforming loans as of March 1999 were estimated by the Financial Supervisory Agency to be 12 percent of total bank lending suggesting little progress in resolving the problem. Japan's infrastructure for the orderly disposal of assets of failed businesses, including financial institutions, was not sufficiently utilized. In December 1999 the deadline for the removal of the blanket deposit guarantee was extended by one year, from

March 2001 to March 2002. This was justified by the Financial Supervisory Agency that time was needed to examine credit cooperatives, whose supervision authorities were being shifted from the prefectural governments to the Financial Supervisory Agency. The Financial Supervisory Agency emphasized in the announcement that bank reform and resolution (as opposed to credit cooperatives) would not be relaxed, and capital injections for banks would be terminated in March 2001 as previously announced. While the one-year extension can be rationalized, it would be a serious mistake to continue the deposit guarantee beyond March 2002. The complex question of government intermediation finance manifested by the Postal Savings System and the Fiscal Investment and Loan Program had only begun to be considered (Cargill and Yoshino 1998, 2000), while at the same time, government financial intermediation increased rather than decreased in importance.

The new and old problems were serious and one would be unrealistic to expect policy to deal with these issues in the short run. What appeared reasonably certain, however, was that Japan had evolved toward a new financial regulation and supervision framework by the end of the decade that would provide a firm basis for sustained economic and financial development in the new century. Banks at the start of 2000 were in a firmer financial condition in terms of capital adequacy and pending mergers than they had been since the late 1980s.

3.4 The New Supervisory and Regulatory Framework

As explained in the six stages, the major Japanese banks were recapitalized and poised to strengthen themselves through strategic mergers and restructuring. The immediate financial crisis had been resolved and the major banks appeared to be on a firmer foundation than at any time since the late 1980s. Japanese regulatory authorities now needed to plan the future agenda.

The blanket deposit guarantee would be replaced by a revised deposit insurance system by 2002. The Financial Supervisory Agency in July 2000 would assume responsibility for financial framework planning, which had previously been the responsibility of the Ministry of Finance. The Financial Supervisory Agency would also be occupied with auditing credit cooperatives from April 2000 on. There will be several, if not many, credit cooperative that will be forced to take drastic steps to remain viable or be closed down. The insurance companies will be also under pressure to restructure, because they have long standing liabilities that promised interest rates much higher than interest rates available in the market in recent years. The immediate focus of the new supervisory and regulatory framework that emerged in 1999 was on the banking system and at the start of the new century, attention would need to be devoted to a wider set of financial issues.

We now consider the new supervisory and regulatory regime that is emerging in Japan from several perspectives: the Financial Supervisory Agency and the Financial Reconstruction Commission, Prompt Corrective Action, the transition to the new financial framework, and the role of the Bank of Japan in the new supervisory regime.

The Financial Supervisory Agency and the Financial Reconstruction Committee

The Financial Supervisory Agency commenced operations in June 1998, concentrating supervision and inspection functions that previously were distributed among at least four different ministries. The new agency is directly under the control of the Prime Minister's office, including appointment of its director general, with the aim toward providing unified supervision towards financial institutions, including agricultural, labor and nonbank institutions. The Agency combines the supervisory sections of the Finance Ministry's Banking Bureau and Securities Bureau as well as the Ministry's Financial Examination section. It also supervises the insurance industry and nonbank financial businesses, such as consumer credit companies, that were formerly under the oversight of the Ministry of International Trade and Industry. The Financial Supervisory Agency also replaces the Ministry of Finance in working with the Ministries of Labor and Agriculture, Forestry, and Fisheries as joint regulators of labor and credit cooperatives.

The Financial Reconstruction Committee established October 1998 further strengthens the relationship between the Financial Supervisory Agency and the Prime Minister. As part of the Office of the Prime Minister, the Financial Reconstruction Committee oversees and supervises the Financial Supervisory Agency.

These institutional changes significantly reduce the influence of the Ministry of Finance, though the Ministry's position will remain important. Since the establishment of the Financial Supervisory Agency, the role of the Ministry of Finance in supervision and regulation has been limited to supervisory framework planning (proposing and drafting new legislation) and with crisis management because it involves fiscal expenditures. After July 2000 the supervisory framework planning function became the responsibility of the Financial Supervisory Agency. While the role of the Ministry of Finance in Japan's financial supervisory and regulatory framework has been reduced, it remains a major force because of its role in fiscal expenditures and crisis management.

Immediately after the establishment of the Financial Supervisory Agency, a number of observers questioned whether the new agency would be independent of the Ministry of Finance. The Ministry, for example, had provided the legislative framework for the new agency and had provided much of the human capital. The first few months of operation, however, showed that the Financial Supervisory agency intended to be independent. The Agency's reputation and independence were greatly enhanced with more transparent reporting of non-performing loans and efforts to temporarily nationalize the Long-Term Credit Bank and Nippon Credit Bank.

Prompt Corrective Action

New procedures for dealing with nonperforming loans and insolvent institutions were established along with deposit insurance reform in 1996. The intent of the new procedures is to deal with bank problems as they arise in a more transparent, systematic and rapid fashion. The Prompt Corrective Action procedures involve two operational areas. The first concerns evaluating and auditing the position of financial institutions, and developing specific measures for supervisors to follow in identifying, correcting, and possibly closing problem financial institutions. More informative and realistic reporting of nonperforming loans illustrates this operational area.

The second operational area concerns the role of supervisors in measuring the position of financial institutions and dealing with problem institutions. The method for calculating capital adequacy ratios has changed to follow international standards more closely. In terms of system management, the objective is to identify problem financial institutions by their capital adequacy ratios, which then trigger specific corrective actions by the supervisors. This is modeled after the "trip wire" system established by the Federal Deposit Insurance Corporation Improvement Act of 1991 in the United States.

The specific implementation of Prompt Corrective Action differs for internationally active and domestically active banks. Internationally active banks are required to maintain an 8 percent capital ratio. Banks with a ratio below 8 percent, but no lower than 4 percent, are required to submit a reform and recapitalization plan to the Financial Supervisory Agency. When the ratio goes below 4 percent, the regulatory oversight and regulatory constraints increase. In addition to forming a recapitalization plan, dividends or executive bonuses must be eliminated or limited and overseas activities and the domestic branch network must be curtailed. When the ratio goes below 2 percent, a substantial reduction in businesses is required and merger or decertification may be encouraged. Some business activities will be suspended when the ratio falls below zero percent. In case of domestically active banks, the same regulatory actions are required as the capital ratio declines; however, the threshold ratios are half of the internationally active banks.

Transition Framework, 1998 to 2002

Japan's supervisory and regulatory framework has been significantly altered by the establishment of the Financial Supervisory Agency and the Financial Reconstruction Commission, reform of the Deposit Insurance Corporation, and Prompt Corrective Action. These new institutions and attitudes will continue to evolve.

Two legislative actions in 1998 (stage five) established a new financial framework: the Law Concerning Emergency Measures for the Reconstruction of the Functions of the Financial System (Financial Reconstruction Law) and the Financial Function Early Restoration Law (Early Restoration Law). Nakaso (1999) provides a succinct discussion of how these legislative actions govern the various roles of regulatory authorities in Japan. The Deposit Insurance Corporation now has three accounts with enhanced resources to deal with troubled institutions: Special Account (17 trillion yen), Financial Reconstruction Account (18 trillion yen), and Account for Early Restoration of Financial Function (25 trillion yen). The Financial Reconstruction Law and enhanced funding made it possible for the regulatory authorities to deal with a bank failure without having to rely on a white knight bank. A failed bank can be temporarily nationalized, or put under supervision of the Financial Reorganization Administrator. The administrator will determine within a year (possibly extended for another year) whether the bank should be liquidated under the Resolution and Collection Corporation or declared a "public bridge bank." If a bridge bank option is chosen (supposedly for a not insolvent institution under supervision of Financial Reorganization Administrator), public capital injection in the form of capital subscription, lending, or loss coverage, can be drawn from Financial Reconstruction Account of the Deposit Insurance Corporation. A temporarily nationalized bank, such as the Long-Term Credit Bank, can receive financial assistance from the Special Account and Financial Reconstruction Account of the Deposit Insurance Corporation.

Weak banks that clear the Prompt Corrective Action standards can apply for a capital injection from the Account for Early Restoration of Financial Function of the Deposit Insurance Corporation, subject to the approval of a business restoration plan. The Financial Reconstruction Commission, which is in charge of approving capital injections, requires that nonperforming loans be disposed of before a bank can receive a capital injection. This was the procedure followed in March 1999.

The Resolution and Collection Corporation was established to assist in the disposal of nonperforming loans. The Resolution and Collection Corporation was established October 1998 and was the outcome of a merger between the Resolution and Collection Bank and Housing Loan Administration Corporation. These two predecessor institutions were previously established as receivers for failed credit cooperatives and remaining assets of the failed housing loan institutions (*jusen*) (Cargill, Hutchison, and Ito 1997). The Resolution and Collection Corporation can now purchase nonperforming loans from solvent operating banks and is charged with ensuring that these transactions are executed at market price or fair value.

The comprehensive safety net established by the Financial Reconstruction Law and the Early Restoration Law is designed to be temporary. The complete deposit guarantee announced in 1995 will be terminated at the end of March 2002. By that time, it is presumed that all banks will be strengthened and the financial distress that characterized Japan for a decade will be a part of Japanese history.

3.5 The Bank of Japan and the New Financial Supervisory and Regulatory Framework

Japan is in the process of fundamental changes in its financial supervisory and regulatory institutions. Further institutional change is possible. The most likely issue with respect to the Bank of Japan will be whether the Bank will retain its current role in the financial supervisory and regulation framework or whether this role will be transferred to the Financial Supervisory Agency along with staff.

There is considerable variation in regard to bank supervision and financial supervision and regulation framework design. Table 3.6 illustrates the range of institutional designs and central bank involvement with bank supervision as of the early 1990s. In table 3.6 (Haubrich 1996; Goodhart and Schoenmaker 1993, 1995), 24 industrial countries are classified according to whether the bank supervision function is part of the country's central bank or outside of the central bank. The table as presented in Haubrich (1996) has been modified to incorporate the recent establishment of the European Central Bank (ECB), changes in the United Kingdom and the addition of South Korea, which also recently revised its central banking law (Cargill 1997–98). Both the United Kingdom and Korea shifted central bank supervision from the central bank, while providing the Bank of England and the Bank of Korea with enhanced formal independence.

Half of the 24 countries listed in table 3.6 separate bank supervision from their central banking institutions. However, table 3.6 needs to be cautiously considered. First, the institutional framework established by legislation does not always reflect the degree of central bank involvement in bank supervision. Central banks without a formal supervisory role may assume such a role as a result of tradition and mutual understanding with other regulatory authorities. In Japan, for example, the Bank of Japan under the pre-1997 legislative framework had no formal role in bank supervision but, over time, evolved an arrangement where it inspected banks on an alternating basis with the Ministry of Finance.

Second, even in those cases where the central bank has no formal role in banking supervision, the central bank is part of the process in evaluating the condition of the banking system and individual banks. It would be hard to imagine a situation where the central bank would be entirely outside of the supervisory process. After all, banks are the counterpart of central bank policy, and central banks will always want to be able to monitor the creditworthiness of their counterpart.

Third, despite the growth of nonbank depositories, nondepository financial institutions, and money and capital markets, central bank supervisory responsibility is almost always focused on the banking system. Liberalization has reduced bank market share in corporate funding and household portfolio management and increased the alliance and consolidation between banks and the rest of the financial system. As a result central banks like the Federal Reserve with a formal supervisory role advocate an expansion of their supervisory function

Table 3.6
Monetary policy and bank supervisory agencies

Country	Monetary policy agency	Bank supervisory agency	Status
Australia	Reserve Bank of Australia	Reserve Bank of Australia	Combined
Austria	National Bank of Austria	Ministry of Finance	Separated
Belgium	National Bank of Belgium	Banking and Finance Commission	Separated
Canada	Bank of Canada	Office of the Superintendent of Financial Institutions	Separated
Denmark	Danmarks Nationalbank	Finance Inspectorate	Separated
Finland	Bank of Finland	Bank Inspectorate, Bank of Finland	Separated
France	Banque de France	Banque de France, Commission Bancaire	Combined
Germany	Deutsche Bundesbank/ECB	Federal Banking Supervisory Office	Separated
Greece	Bank of Greece	Bank of Greece	Combined
Hong Kong	Hong Kong Monetary Authority	Hong Kong Monetary Authority	Combined
Ireland	Central Bank of Ireland/ECB	Central Bank of Ireland	Combined
Italy	Banca d'Italia	Banca d'Italia	Combined
Japan	Bank of Japan	Ministry of Finance, Bank of Japan	Separated
Luxembourg	Luxembourg Monetary Institute/ECB	Luxembourg Monetary Institute	Combined
Mexico	Banco de Mexico	National Banking and Securities Commission	Separated
Netherlands	De Nederlandsche Bank/ECB	De Nederlandsche Bank	Combined
New Zealand	Reserve Bank of New Zealand	Reserve Bank of New Zealand	Combined
Norway	Norges Bank	Banking, Insurance and Securities Commission	Separated
Portugal	Banco de Portugal/ECB	Banco de Portugal	Combined
Spain	Banco de Espana/ECB	Banco de Espana	Combined
South Korea	Bank of Korea	Financial Supervision Commission	Separated
Sweden	Sveriges Riksbank	Swedish Financial Supervisory Authority	Separated
Switzerland	Swiss National Bank	Federal Banking Commission	Separated
United Kingdom	Bank of England		Separated
United States	Federal Reserve System	Federal Reserve System, OCC, FDIC, state governments	Combined

Source: Haubrich (1996, p. 3) with modifications for the European Central Bank (ECB), South Korea, and the United Kingdom.

to these new areas of the financial system. In fact, debate over the future supervisory role of the Federal Reserve has slowed the process of liberalization in the United States. Failure to pass bank modernization legislation has as much to do with regulatory turf battles between the Federal Reserve and the Treasury as it does over the merits of whether banks should be granted powers to underwrite securities and/or insurance policies.

Central Banks and Bank Supervision

Irrespective of institutional design, central banks generally play an advisory role in the supervisory process. The substantive debate, however, focuses on whether central banks should have a formal role in the process. The arguments for each side are well known (e.g., Haubrich 1996; Goodhart and Schoenmaker 1993, 1995; International Monetary Fund 1995)

There are three arguments in support of a formal role for central bank supervision. First, the central bank possess the specialized human capital to assume the supervisory function. Its human capital, at least, equals and likely exceeds the human capital of any other regulatory agency and is derived from the central bank's conduct of monetary policy. Second, the central bank cannot be expected to be an effective lender of last resort unless it has accurate, detailed, and timely information on the condition of the banking system in general, and individual banks in particular. Third, the knowledge obtained via playing an active supervisory role not only contributes to more effective lender of last resort but also contributes to more overall effective monetary policy. Detailed knowledge of the banking system's condition can be taken into account in how aggressively to use the general policy instruments such as open market operations.

There are three counter arguments to a formal supervisory role assigned to the central bank. First, the human capital needed for bank supervision is not unique to the central bank, nor is it clear that regulatory agencies in general are able to assess bank risk better than the market (Berger and Davies 1998; Cargill 1989). Second, there are potential conflicts between monetary policy and supervision in that the central bank becomes "captured" by the industry it supervises. As a result, for example, the central bank may be reluctant to aggressively raise interest rates. This in fact may have been the case in the United States in the 1970s when the Federal Reserve used monetary policy in a failed

attempt to maintain low interest rates so as not to induce disintermediation because of Regulation Q interest rate ceilings (Mayer 1982). The
result was a period of disruptive inflation. Third, monetary policy in
the pursuit of price stability should not concern itself with the health of
a specific sector of the economy. Lender of last resort exists as a safety
valve to ensure that localized bank problems do not spread. Moreover
the stability of the banking system is more a function of well-designed
deposit guarantee systems, sufficient capital-asset ratios, and overall
price stability than direct central banking intervention in the banking
system.

Clearly, the issue has been decided differently from country to country. Three developments, however, suggest that a less formal role in
bank supervision may be the more desirable direction in Japan. In
order to consider the role of a central bank in supervision, three developments seem important: increasing emphasis on political and operational independence, financial liberalization, and financial distress.

Central Bank Independence
Central bank institutional design is increasingly directed toward providing the central bank with legal, practical operating, and policy formulation independence. Central banks also need to be independent of
the banking system or any other sector of the financial system over
which it may have supervisory or regulatory responsibility. The public
choice literature emphasizes that agency problems are likely to arise
between a regulatory authority and the regulated entity so that regulatory policy becomes adverse to the general public.

Financial Liberalization
Financial liberalization has widened and deepened the financial system, thus suggesting that supervision of different sectors be concen-
trated into one agency. Financial liberalization has also elevated the
need to develop new supervisory and regulatory policies such as
Prompt Corrective Action to minimize the need for lender of last
resort. Higher capital-asset ratios on banks, making banks more dependent on raising funds in the capital market through subordinate
debt, risk-adjusted deposit insurance premiums, lower deposit insurance limits, "trip wire" systems to limit regulatory discretion are exam-
ples of policies that carry out this objective. Lender of last resort is not
eliminated by these procedures, but it should become less important
over time. Thus, financial liberalization has weakened the argument

made by central banks that they should be active players in bank supervision. Banks will likely continue to lose market share to other depository institutions and the successful adoption of new regulatory procedures will reduce the role of lender of last resort.

There is another liberalization perspective that suggests a reduced role for central bank supervision of the banking industry. Banks have consistently lost market share to nonbank financial institutions and capital markets as liberalization has progressed. This has been true to a limited extent in Japan; however, according to Hoshi and Kashyap (1999) and other analysts, Japan is likely to experience a significant decline in the role of banking in the near future. This provides an additional argument for the need to separate central banks from the banking system so central banks can begin to develop a broader perspective of monetary policy in a more diverse financial system.

Financial Distress
Politicians and regulatory authorities have exhibited a common pattern in dealing with financial stress that ultimately involves some form of forbearance and forgiveness. This policy response has the potential to impose considerable pressure on central banks to support weak financial institutions until they "work their way out of the problem." Those central banks that have a formal supervisory responsibility over the banking system can easily become conflicted over its responsibility for broad monetary policy objectives and concern for its constituency among financial sector participants. Central banks without a formal supervisory role are also likely to be pressured, though less likely to adopt a protective attitude toward the banking system.

The New Bank of Japan's Role in Financial Supervision, Regulation, and Maintaining Orderly Financial Markets

As discussed in the next chapter, the new Bank of Japan is assigned two responsibilities: price stability and an orderly credit and payments system. The evolution of the new financial supervision and regulation framework to date has not had much impact on the Bank of Japan. The new Bank of Japan remains a lender of last resort and an important contributor to discussions of how best to deal with Japan's financial distress and future liberalization. The Bank of Japan also continues to supervise private-sector banks.

The new framework has two implications for the Bank of Japan. First, further institutional change may require that the current Bank of Japan supervisory responsibilities be transferred to the Financial Supervisory Agency. The arguments against such an institutional change are difficult to deflect, especially as financial liberalization changes the structure of the financial system and reduces the market share of banking in corporate funding and household portfolio management. Second, the new financial supervision and regulation framework, if successfully developed and implemented, will reduce pressure on the Bank of Japan to actively use its lender of last resort power. The modern approach is to devise a framework that provides for an orderly process of dealing with troubled institutions before they pose a constraint on monetary policy.

3.6 Concluding Comments

The events that brought Japan to an economic and financial crisis described in chapter 2, were rooted in an old financial supervision and regulation framework. The old framework came into increasing conflict with new economic, political, and technological forces in the 1990s. These conflicts were not unique to Japan. The old financial supervision and regulation framework in the United States, for example, resisted change and ultimately led to the collapse of the S&L industry and banking problems in the late 1980s and early 1990s (Benston and Kaufman 1997). Japan is special, however, in the resistance the old regime has exhibited. While Japan was quickly becoming a major participant in an increasingly integrated world economic and financial order, it attempted to retain a regime of supervision and regulation more appropriate for a closed economy.

Six identifiable stages outline the steps that have been taken in Japan during the 1990s to shift from the old to a new financial supervision and regulation regime. The new regime is being achieved with both institutional and policy changes based on the recognition that delay, moral hazard, lack of transparency, and unwillingness to impose penalties ultimately increases the cost of resolving financial problems, both in economic and political terms.

4   The New Bank of Japan

4.1   Introduction

The legal aspects of a central bank are important because they codify the central bank's objectives, responsibilities, relationship with the government, and other institutional matters. Well-designed central bank legislation establishes a framework that enables the central bank to pursue those responsibilities for which it is designed. Price stability and lender of last resort services are accepted central bank responsibilities, while there is less consensus regarding other responsibilities such as short-term macroeconomic stabilization, financial regulation, and supervision.

Irrespective of differences of opinion over central bank responsibilities, the objective of central bank legislation in recent years has been to establish a framework that enables the central bank to pursue its responsibilities as an authorized corporation without pressure from various branches of government. These pressures, especially pressure to pursue easy monetary policy, might conflict with the ultimate responsibilities of the central bank. Insulation to conduct policy is achieved by institutional design, which provides the central bank with formal and legal independence to pursue monetary policy.

The legal foundation of the Bank of Japan was revised by legislation passed in June 1997 and became effective April 1, 1998. The revised Bank of Japan Law will be referred to as the 1998 Bank of Japan Law or the 1998 Law. The new Bank of Japan will be referred to as the 1998 Bank of Japan. The 1998 designation is based on the fact that the 1997 legislation became effective in 1998. The 1998 Law was the first major institutional change in the Bank of Japan since 1942. The new Law is a major departure from the 1942 Law as well as earlier versions of the Law in terms of central bank objectives, responsibilities, and relationship with the government. The differences in the new Law compared to the 1942 and earlier Laws are sufficiently significant that we can now refer to the "new" Bank of Japan as opposed to the "old" Bank of Japan. The institutional change is designed to provide the Bank of Japan with greater formal, operational, and political independence.

The 1942 Law rendered the Bank of Japan one of the world's most formally dependent central banks. Table 4.1 summarizes the rankings of central bank independence for 17 industrialized countries taken from several studies as of 1993. Each country's central bank is ranked on the Cukierman, Webb, and Neyapti (1993) index from the most independent to the least independent central bank with other independence measures indicated for that country. The Bank of Japan based on the 1942 Law was clearly regarded as a formally dependent central bank.[1]

The 1998 Law is significant from at least three perspectives. First, the 1998 Law significantly enhanced the legal independence of the Bank of Japan from the Ministry of Finance and freed it from the constraints imposed by the "wartime" version of the 1942 Law.

Second, the Bank of Japan's independence ranking such as presented in table 4.1 needs to be revised since all of the generally available cross-country rankings have been based on the 1942 Law for the Bank of Japan. Revision of the Bank of Japan index will assist in determining the degree to which the Bank of Japan's legal independence has been enhanced.

Third, the 1998 revision is part of a broad institutional restructuring process initiated in 1995 and already discussed in chapter 3. Revision of the Bank of Japan Law is part of this process of institutional change and thus needs to be considered in the broader context of a transition

---

1. The various studies are not consistent in their ranking of the Bank of Japan, although in general, the Bank of Japan is regarded as one of the more formally dependent central banks among the industrialized countries. Cukierman, Webb, and Neyapti regard the Bank of Japan as one of the least independent central banks in the world. According to their ranking of 72 countries for the 1980 to 1989 period, only Belgium, Morocco, Poland, Norway, and Yugoslavia had more dependent central banks than Japan and Nepal was tied with Japan.

In contrast, the Bade–Parkin–Alesina index (modification and extension of the original Bade and Parkin 1982 ranking and reported in Alesina and Summers 1993) assign the Bank of Japan a relatively high level of independence. They attribute as much independence to the Bank of Japan as to the Federal Reserve, which most would regard as one of the more independent central banks in the world. Burdekin and Willett (1991) and Cargill (1989, 1993a, 1995) specifically criticize Japan's high independence ranking based on the 1942 Law.

Table 4.1
Central bank independence index values: Industrial economies

Country	CWN[a]	BPA[b]	GMT[c]	BWW[d]	ES[e]
Germany	0.69	4	13	3	5
Switzerland	0.64	4	12	3	5
Austria	0.61	NA	NA	2	3
Denmark	0.50	2	8	NA	4
United States	0.48	3	12	2	3
Canada	0.45	2	11	1	1
Ireland	0.44	NA	NA	NA	NA
Netherlands	0.42	2	10	1	4
Australia	0.36	1	9	1	1
Iceland	0.34	NA	NA	NA	NA
Luxembourg	0.33	NA	NA	NA	NA
Sweden	0.29	2	NA	1	2
Finland	0.28	NA	NA	NA	3
United Kingdom	0.27	2	6	1	3
Italy	0.25	1.5	5	1	2
New Zealand	0.24	1	3	1	3
France	0.24	2	7	1	2
Spain	0.23	1	5	NA	3
Japan	0.18	3	6	1	3
Norway	0.17	2	NA	NA	2
Belgium	0.17	2	7	1	3

Note: Higher values of the index indicate greater formal independence. Countries are ranked according to the CWN index. NA = not assigned an independent index.
a. Cukierman, Webb, and Neyapti (1993, p. 362): 1980–1989 period, 1.0 to 0.0 scale.
b. Bade-Parkin-Alesina (1982) reported in Alesina and Summers (1993, p. 154): 1973–1988 period, 4 to 1.0 point scale.
c. Grilli, Masciandaro, and Tabellini (1991) index reported in Alesina and Summers (1993, p. 154): 1973–1988 period, 13 to 1 point scale.
d. Burdekin, Wihlborg, and Willett (1992, p. 235): 1960–1989 period, 3 to 1 point scale.
e. Eijffinger and Schaling (1993): a 10-year period, 5 to 1 scale.

from an "old" to a "new" financial supervision and regulation framework.

4.2   The Old Bank of Japan

The Bank of Japan was established in October 1882 to be the sole issuer of convertible notes in response to the failure of the national banking system to limit the supply of bank notes.[2] The Bank of Japan from the outset was under the direction of the Ministry of Finance and was formally organized as a corporation with 55 percent of its capital provided by the government and 45 percent of its capital provided by the private sector.

The Bank of Japan's license was extended in 1910, to become effective in 1912, for another thirty years. There were only minor differences between the 1882 and 1912 Law. The Law was revised in 1942 in the midst of World War II. Differences between the "wartime" Law and the early versions of the Law are often exaggerated;[3] however, the 1942 Law did render the Bank of Japan more dependent on the government than previously because of its explicit requirement that the Bank of Japan support the war effort. The 1942 Law, with a modification in

---

2. An English translation of the 1882 Law is available in the "Japan Times" Office (1902). English translations of the 1910, 1942, and 1998 Laws cited in this book were provided by the Institute of Monetary and Economic Studies, Bank of Japan.

3. The wartime conditions of the 1942 Law are frequently exaggerated. In fact comparison of the 1882 and 1942 Laws reveals little difference in the expressed relationship between the Bank of Japan and the government. While the 1942 Law was more explicit in defining the responsibility of the Bank of Japan to support the national economy, the 1942 Law was not a significant change in this regard. Selected articles from the 1882 Law and its By-laws illustrate this point.

"The Bank of Japan is empowered to issue convertible bank notes; provided that, when permission to exercise this privilege is given, the Government shall enact special rules related to the same." (Article 14)

"The Bank of Japan shall make a report to the Minister of State for Finance at least once a month, stating in detail the actual condition of the business conducted by the head office, branches and correspondents." (Article 22)

"The Government shall oversee the management of all the business of the Bank of Japan, and shall be competent to interdict not only all transactions at variance with the provisions of the Bank of Japan Act and the By-laws, but also such as, in the government opinions, may seem disadvantageous." (Article 86)

"The Government may, if it deem necessary, revise or amend these By-laws at any time." (Article 87)

Thus, while the 1942 Law clarified the specific role of the Bank of Japan to use its control over credit "for national aims," the essential relationship between the Bank of Japan and the government remained unchanged between the 1882 and 1942 Law.

1949 in response to a reform effort by the Allied Occupation Force after the war, remained the institutional and legal framework for the Bank of Japan until 1998 despite occasional calls for revision. In fact it seems unusual the 1942 Law survived the period of democratization and reform after the war, whereas Germany revised its central banking institutions shortly after the war.

The 1942 Law

The 1942 Law charged the Bank of Japan with conducting its operations "... in order that the general economic activities of the nation might adequately be enhanced" (Article 1) and that "the Bank of Japan shall be managed solely for achievement of national aims (Article 2)." The phrase "national aims" can be interpreted in terms of supporting military objectives during wartime and supporting potential economic growth during peacetime. There was no specific reference to financial stability, price stability, or any other standard central bank responsibility. These objectives, however, as well as almost any objective decreed important by the government, were covered by the broad mission statement of the 1942 Law.

The Bank of Japan was placed under the direction of the Ministry of Finance in virtually every important respect according the 1942 Law.[4] The Bank of Japan was intended to be an instrument of government policy as interpreted by the Minister of Finance, which could just as easily be interpreted for peacetime as well as wartime conditions.

---

4. The Ministry had major oversight responsibility of Bank of Japan operations and staffing. The Bank of Japan could establish branches, additional offices, or secure agents to carry out its operations only with the permission of the Minister (Article 4). The chief operating officers of the Bank of Japan (Governor, Vice-Governor, and a number of Executive Directors, Auditors, and Advisers) were either appointed by, or subject to approval by the Minister (Article 16). Bank note issue was subject to a limit determined by the Cabinet, and note issues in excess of the limit required the approval of the Ministry (Articles 30 and 31). The Bank of Japan could be required to provide uncollateralized loans to the government (Articles 22 and 23) and with the permission of the Minster "... undertake such businesses as are necessary for the maintenance and fostering of the credit system." (Article 25). The influence of the Ministry of Finance in Bank of Japan operations extended to the private sector in that the Minister "... whenever deemed necessary ... [could] order banks and other financial institutions to cooperate in the execution of the business of the Bank of Japan (Article 28)." The Bank of Japan was placed under the supervision of the Minister (Article 42) which had the power to order the "... Bank to undertake any necessary business, or order alternatives in the By-Laws as well as other necessary actions (Article 43)."

Modifications to the 1942 Bank of Japan Law

Two modifications to the Law were made in 1947 and 1949 and several attempts were made at various times in the postwar period to initiate a more fundamental revision of the Law.

The first modification was not to the Bank of Japan Law per se but an outcome of the 1947 Finance Law that provided the Bank of Japan with a degree of independence from government deficit financing. The Bank of Japan had supported government deficits shortly after the war by monetization of government bonds that resulted in triple digit inflation rates in 1946, 1947, and 1948.

The Finance Law clarified limits on the use of the Bank of Japan to underwrite government bonds. The Finance Law prohibited the Bank of Japan from underwriting government bonds. The Bank of Japan adopted an internal policy not to purchase government bonds within a year of their issuance. The Finance Law, however, permitted the Bank of Japan to underwrite short-term Finance Bills discussed below. The Finance Law prohibits the Bank of Japan from underwriting or making loans to the government with some exceptions. Underwriting can occur if the amount of the underwriting or the loan is authorized by the Diet and if it is done under special circumstances. This exception has been interpreted to mean that the Bank of Japan can underwrite government bonds issued to refinance maturing debt (up to an amount authorized by the Diet).

In 1949 the Bank of Japan Law was amended to establish a Policy Board designed to provide overall management of the Bank of Japan. The Policy Board was composed of five voting and two nonvoting members. The Policy Board was given final responsibility for virtually every monetary and nonmonetary policy operation of the Bank of Japan. The five voting members included the governor of the Bank of Japan and four persons appointed by the Cabinet representing large city banks, regional banks, commerce and industry, and agriculture. In practice, executives from a large city and regional bank and retired officials from the Ministry of Agriculture, Forestry, and Fishery and the Ministry of International Trade and Industry were appointed. The two nonvoting members consisted of a representative of the Ministry of Finance and the Economic Planning Agency. The voting members selected the chair of the Policy Board.

The dominance of the Ministry of Finance over the Bank of Japan remained intact however, despite the new Policy Board. The articles of the Bank of Japan Law that gave the Ministry of Finance complete control over the Bank of Japan and the ability to influence, if not outright determine, policy decisions of the Policy Board remained in place.

The Policy Board had the potential to become the main policy-making body of the Bank of Japan and even to provide the Bank of Japan with greater practical independence despite the wording of the 1942 Law. However, this did not occur. The Policy Board lapsed into the practice of following the recommendations made by Bank of Japan staff or an executive board of directors representing several departments within the Bank of Japan.

There were several public discussions over the next forty years to revise the 1942 Law. The most extensive occurred in the early 1960s. These discussions focused on changes that would have provided the Bank of Japan with some legal independence from the Ministry of Finance. However, the degree of independence that would have resulted is not entirely clear.

In the late 1950s the Committee on Financial System Research debated the proper relationship between the Bank of Japan and the government. An intense debate was summarized in a report submitted in 1960 to the Minister of Finance. The debate was framed in terms of two plans (Shionoya 1962; Suzuki 1987, pp. 314–15) for resolving conflicts between the Bank of Japan and the Ministry of Finance. Plan A required the Bank of Japan to simply follow the instructions of the Ministry as long as they did not violate the guiding principles of the Bank of Japan. Plan B limited the Ministry to a request for postponement of a policy for a certain period of time while the Bank of Japan independently acted. Despite considerable discussion the issue was never resolved, and the Bank of Japan remained formally under the influence of the 1942 Bank of Japan Law.

The debate over plans A and B represented the most serious effort prior to 1998 to revise the 1942 Law. Revision was subsequently discussed at various times, but revision of the Law was a low priority for the Ministry of Finance who saw no compelling political or economic rationale to alter the legal foundation of the Bank of Japan.

4.3   The Need for Central Bank Independence in Japan

The Bank of Japan, despite its legal dependence on the Ministry of Finance and constraints imposed by the "wartime" conditions of the 1942 Law, achieved a successful policy record for much of the postwar period. The price stabilization record of the Bank of Japan, combined with the sustained real growth of the Japanese economy over the 1975 to 1985 period in particular, attracted international attention to the Bank of Japan. The Bank of Japan appeared to contradict the conventional wisdom that legally independent central banks generate the best price stability records.

Cargill, Hutchison, and Ito (1997) explain this contradiction. It may be that the Bank of Japan gained de facto independence after the experience of the high inflation rates in the early 1970s and the first oil crisis in 1973. An important episode during this period was that the government overruled the Bank of Japan's request to raise the discount rate in 1972. Inflation soared in 1973. The Bank of Japan was then in a position to cite this episode to support their position in any debate with the Ministry of Finance over monetary policy. As the Bank of Japan established the reputation of a price stabilizing central bank, especially after the second oil crisis, de facto independence seemed to have been established. Another hypothesis is that the Ministry of Finance shielded the Bank of Japan from political pressure as a benevolent intermediary.

The role of reputation in explaining central bank policy outcomes can be formalized; however, these models are characterized by multiple equilibrium solutions. Economic and/or political shocks can destabilize the system, moving the economy from a low to a high-inflation discretionary situation. This result has been illustrated at least twice in Japan's postwar economy. Economic and political shocks destabilized the reputational constraint on inflationary monetary policy in the early 1970s and the second half of the 1980s.

The political and economic situation changed in the second half of the 1980s and early 1990s suggesting that these types of shocks are more likely. The political stability achieved by the single-party dominance of the LDP from 1955 to 1992 ended in 1993 and is not likely to reemerge anytime soon. The LDP lost its majority position in the Lower House (House of Representatives) in August 1993, and while in October 1996, the LDP with coalition partners regained some of its strength by winning 230 of the 511 Lower House seats, it still fell short of a majority. However, by creating a coalition, the LDP was able to form the government. The new political structure suggests that Japanese politics will be more fractionalized with more competing groups seeking power through coalition tactics.

This political change has taken place at the same time Japan has experienced its most severe financial and economic crisis in the postwar period. Stagnation in the 1990s, financial distress, declining output in 1998, and the very slow recovery in 1999 compounded by an aging population provide incentives for politicians to distinguish themselves by offering different social, political, and economic policies. This will likely increase incentives for any incumbent party to exploit the short-run Phillips curve to increase the probability of retaining and enhancing power. Even during the pre-1993 period when the LDP-dominated Japanese politics and economic conditions were mostly positive, political business cycle interactions could be identified (Cargill, Hutchison, and Ito 1997). The recent structural changes in Japan's political system are likely to enhance the interaction between political institutions and macroeconomic activity.

Thus the political and economic changes taking place in Japan during the past decade increased the likelihood that reputation for price stability would be insufficient to ensure proper central bank policy. It was time for the Bank of Japan to be given greater political independence to minimize the probability that monetary policy will become an instrument of any one of several competing factions. Thus, while the Bank of Japan was able to achieve price stability despite its formal and legal dependence on the government during much of the postwar period, the conditions that permitted this policy outcome were eroding.

4.4 The New Bank of Japan

In 1996 Prime Minister Hashimoto formed a special "study group" for reforming the Bank of Japan. Between July and November the group had intensive discussions and produced a report calling for enhanced independence. The Ministry of Finance seemed to have cooperated fully in this effort. This stood in sharp contrast to the Ministry's position prior to 1996. What events moved revision of the 1942 Law to the forefront, how did the revision process evolve so as to establish consensus, and what are the features of the new Bank of Japan as specified by the 1998 Law?

The Environment for Revision

Revision of the institutional design of the Bank of Japan shifted to a high-profile policy issue in 1996 in response to the combined influence of events external and internal to Japan. The external events provided an environment favorable for institutional change, but the internal events were key to the revision of the 1942 Law.

External influences elevated the discussion of central bank independence in Japan. Consensus had been reached by the late 1970s that substantial long-lasting inflation was almost always associated with excessive money growth. As such, the institutional design of the central bank needed to ensure that the central bank's technical control over the money supply would contribute to price stability. In the opinion of many, legal independence was an important element of this design. Financial liberalization in the 1980s also provided an incentive to reconsider central bank institutional design, especially in developing countries or countries established by the breakup of the Soviet Union. Financial distress experienced by many countries in the late 1980s and early 1990s also intensified discussions about the institutional design of the financial system and as part of these discussions, central bank institutional design.

Revision of the 1942 Law, however, would not have likely become a reality in the absence of a series of economic and political events within Japan. These included the growing public dissatisfaction with the Ministry of Finance's handling of the nonperforming loan problem, the weakened relationship between the LDP and the Ministry of Finance during the three-year period the LDP was not in control of the Lower House, and the need to accelerate Japan's financial liberalization agenda.

The reputation of the Ministry of Finance was weakened by its failure to deal with the nonperforming loan problem in the early 1990s. The reputation was further weakened in 1995 when the *jusen* industry was liquidated and other disclosures indicated the Ministry of Finance had grossly understated the magnitude of nonperforming loans.

The November 1996 announcement of the Big Bang financial reforms was a genuine policy response to long overdue structural reforms in the Japanese financial system. At the same time the Big Bang was viewed as an opportune political platform for the LDP that had regained control of the Lower House in October 1996 with the aid of coalition parties. The traditionally strong relationship between the Ministry of Finance and the LDP weakened from 1993 to 1996 as the Ministry turned its support to the new parties in power. Thus, once returned to power, the LDP and Prime Minister Hashimoto were willing to undertake reforms opposed by the Ministry of Finance in the context of growing public dissatisfaction with the Ministry of Finance.

The resulting Big Bang legislation in the spring of 1997 included significant institutional change in Japan's supervision and regulatory framework that reduced the role of the Ministry of Finance. The Financial Supervisory Agency was established to take over many of the supervision and regulatory functions of the Ministry with respect to banks, other depositories, and securities markets. The Bank of Japan Law was revised to grant legal independence from the Ministry of Finance.

Some argued the asset inflation and subsequent collapse of asset prices illustrated the need to separate the Bank of Japan from the Ministry of Finance. In particular, the Bank of Japan was frequently blamed for creating a "bubble" economy in the second half of the 1980s. The Bank of Japan expanded the monetary base to limit yen appreciation and maintain an expanding economy while the Ministry continued with deficit reduction. Ueda (2000), one of the five appointed members to the Policy Board established by the 1998 Law, holds this view. Ueda implies that had the Bank of Japan been more independent, it would have been less likely to have followed such an expansionary policy.

The Ministry of Finance was less than enthusiastic about either of the institutional changes legislated in spring 1997. In order to direct attention away from its past policy failures, however, the Ministry became an active supporter of central bank independence (*Wall Street Journal*, August 2, 1996) in late 1996.

Consensus Building and the Revision Process

By the 1990s it became increasingly clear that the Bank of Japan's legal foundation was at odds with those in most other industrial economies. As the central bank of the world's second largest economy it had gained considerable credibility as a price stabilizing central bank despite its formal dependence on the Ministry of Finance (Cargill 1989, 1993a; Cargill, Hutchison, and Ito 1997). Revision of the 1942 Law, if for no other reason than to disassociate Japan from a war five decades in the past, seemed long overdue.

The external and internal influences provided an environment favorable to revising the 1942 Law toward more legal independence for the Bank of Japan, including support for revision from the Ministry of Finance. Motivation of the Ministry of Finance, however, is a minor footnote to the issue of central bank independence in Japan. The real issue is whether the times called for a more formally independent central bank and whether the change in institutional design will provide the Bank of Japan with the flexibility needed to deal with what Lohmann (1997) calls the "new Japan."

The first step was to establish consensus for such a major institutional change. In this regard the leadership role played by Prime Minister Hashimoto and the concurrence of the Ministry of Finance played an important role in the consensus building process, even though the support of the Ministry of Finance was not enthusiastic.

In 1996 Prime Minister Hashimoto appointed an eight-member private advisory committee headed by Keio University President Yasuhiko Torii to report on revising the 1942 Law. The view of the Group is clearly expressed by the title of their November 12, 1996, report: "Reform of the Central Bank System—In Pursuit of "Open Independence.""[5]

The report contains seven sections dealing with specific aspects of Bank of Japan policy, a section dealing with miscellaneous issues, and a concluding section. A brief summary of the report follows:

1. Introduction. The 1942 Bank of Japan Law is outdated and needs to be revised. The structure of the Bank of Japan needs to be changed to provide more transparency for monetary policy, both within Japan as financial markets become more competitive and open and outside of Japan, as the Bank of Japan needs to maintain and enhance credibility. This will be accomplished by securing independence for the Bank of Japan which has been found to be a necessary condition for monetary policy and is being considered in the context of the European Monetary Union. The specific type of independence for the Bank of Japan is referred to as "open independence."

2. Objectives of the Bank of Japan. The Bank of Japan has two responsibilities: price stability and maintaining an orderly credit and payment system. Price stability is the most important objective for the Bank of Japan while maintaining an orderly credit system is the ultimate responsibility of the government.

3. "Open independence." The role of the Policy Board should be elevated to be the primary decision making body for monetary policy. The government will continue to play a role through the authority to nom-

---

5. The version of the report used for this paper is a provisional translation by the Bank of Japan.

inate Policy Board members; however, the government's broad power to give orders to the Bank of Japan should be abolished. The Bank of Japan in turn needs to be transparent to the public and the government —independence with transparency or "open independence."

4. How to secure transparency and accountability. The Policy Board's summary discussions should be made public after a certain period of time with the full transcript made public after a considerable period of time. In addition the Bank of Japan needs to find methods to explain monetary policy decisions to the public and the Diet.

5. Strengthening the Policy Board. The ultimate authority of the Policy Board needs to be reinstated. Important monetary policy decisions had de facto come to be made at the Bank executive meetings and efforts need to be made to reestablish the authority of the Policy Board. The Policy Board should assume responsibility for both monetary policy and policies regarding the Bank of Japan's business operations. Policy Board meetings should be publicly scheduled. Membership on the Policy Board should consist of some Bank of Japan executives, the governor, and outside monetary experts selected for their expertise and not to represent a specific sector of the economy. Bank executives should not constitute a majority of the Policy Board. The government retains the right to have government-designated individuals attend Policy Board meetings; however, they will have no voting rights.

6. Relationship between the Bank of Japan and the government. The relationship with government differs according to three specific function of the Bank of Japan. Independence from government is required for monetary policy, government involvement is required for dealing with financial instability, and government responsibility is required in foreign exchange intervention and management of government funds.

In the case of a difference of opinion between the Bank of Japan and the government, the government has the right to make its view known to the Policy Board, including the right of the government to request that the Policy Board postpone a decision for a period of time.

7. Business operations of the Bank of Japan. The Bank of Japan as a "banker of banks" conducts monetary policy as its intrinsic duty. The Bank of Japan is also a fiscal agent for the government as a "bank of government." The Bank of Japan plays a role in maintaining an orderly credit system and on-site examinations of financial institutions. In regard to actions to ensure the stability of financial markets and institutions, the government has the ultimate responsibility because of the

role of administrative guidance in such situations. The Bank of Japan, however, will play an important role as a lender of last resort either under the direction of the government with due regard for moral hazard or on its own initiative. The government is to be involved in cases of dealing with international financial crisis or exchange rate policies; however, the Bank of Japan should be allowed to conduct foreign exchange operations on its own initiative.

8. Other issues. Bank of Japan executives and staff should be subject to secrecy requirements given the confidential nature of their business, the current corporate structure of the Bank of Japan where 55 percent of capital is government owned and 45 percent private owned is satisfactory, and audits, and oversight of Bank of Japan operations should not interfere with monetary policy independence.

9. Conclusion. "Open independence" is required for the Bank of Japan to play the role as "a central bank capable of becoming the nucleus of the financial system in the 21st century." Institution change, however, is only a necessary but not sufficient condition to gain credibility with the public and the global community.

The Committee's November 1996 report was reviewed by the Financial System Study Committee, an advisory committee to the Ministry of Finance chaired by Ryuichiro Tachi, professor emeritus at the University of Tokyo. This was part of the formality to form a consensus among vested interest groups according to long established traditions in Japan. The Financial System published their report February 6, 1997, and closely followed the November 1996 report.

The recommendations were debated in the Diet during spring 1997 and in June, the 1942 Law was revised to become effective April 1, 1998. The Bank of Japan remained silent in public, although behind the scene, negotiations between the Bank of Japan and the Ministry of Finance were intense. The Bank of Japan's public silence has led some (Mikitani and Kuwayama 1998, p. 3) to argue the Bank of Japan was passive during the process leading to the 1998 Law.

4.5   The 1998 Bank of Japan Law

The 1998 Law can be summarized in comparative perspective to the 1942 Law by considering the following topics: central bank objective, formal relationship (independence) to government, policy-making process, transparency and accountability, budgeting, special uncollateralized loans, exchange rate operations, bank supervision, bank note issues, and government financing. Table 4.2 presents a summary comparison of key differences between the old and new Bank of Japan Law.

Central Bank Objective

The Bank of Japan under the old law was required to conduct its control over the credit system so "... that the general economic activities of the nation might adequately be enhanced. (Article 1)." This objective was so broadly defined that almost any policy action pursued by the Bank of Japan was consistent with the 1942 Law's central bank objective. In practice, however, the Bank of Japan after 1973 directed policy toward achieving price stability.

The 1998 Law specifies two operating principles for the Bank of Japans to be followed in implementing currency and monetary control: "the pursuit of price stability, contributing to the sound development of the national economy (Article 2)," and "maintenance of an orderly financial system (Article 1)." Price stability is not specifically defined nor specified as the only policy objective. The absence of references to full employment, economic growth, or exchange rate objectives, however, suggests that price stability at least from an operational perspective is the primary goal of monetary policy along with stability of the financial system. The new Law clearly states that the Bank of Japan is responsible for price stability while the responsibility for financial stability is a shared responsibility with government.

The 1998 Law assumes that price stability and financial stability (lender of last resort) objectives will not conflict, nor does the new Law specify price stability. The Law does not mention an inflation target, but it does not preclude an inflation target either. Thus, while the objectives of the Bank of Japan were narrowed from those of the 1942 Law, there remains room for interpretation as to the meaning of price stability and how price stability will contribute "... to the sound development of the national economy."

Formal Relationship (Independence) to the Government

The old Law stated explicitly that the Bank of Japan was an instrument of the Ministry of Finance and government in virtually every area of operation. This was most clearly expressed by the authority granted to the Cabinet to dismiss the governor and vice-governor and for the

Table 4.2
Summary comparison between the old and new Bank of Japan law

Old	New	Comments
Objectives		
To promote full potential of the economy (Articles 1 and 2)	Pursuit of price stability, contributing to sound development of national economy (Article 2)	Exchange rate is not mentioned. Contributing to sound development of the national economy is mentioned.
	Maintenance of orderly financial system (Article 1)	Price stability as a sole objective is denied.
Independence		
Ministry of Finance had power for a wide range of businesses (Article 43)	Ministry of Finance power to direct businesses removed	Independence is enhanced.
Cabinet could dismiss the governor (Article 47)	Governor cannot be dismissed due to the difference in opinion (Article 24)	
Policy Board ("double board")		
Important issues decided in Executive Board; Policy Board did not discuss issues deeply	Board consists of nine persons (governor of the Bank of Japan, 2 deputy governors, and 6 deliberative members) (Article 16)	Government members are no longer Board members. Their requests for delaying decisions can be overruled.
Policy Board composed of 1 governor; 4 members representing financial businesses, agriculture, and commerce	In-house Executive Board abolished	
Government (Ministry of Finance and Economic Planning Agency) had two representatives on the Board that did not have voting power	Broad range of power given to the Policy Board (Article 15)	
	Government representative (Ministry of Finance and Economic Planning Agency) can attend meetings, express opinions, and request the delay of decision (Article 19)	

Transparency and accountability	Disclosure and transparency implemented "to clarify to the public the content of its decisions, as well as its decision making process, regarding currency and monetary control" (Article 3)	Accountability to the Diet is enhanced.
	Publication of minutes (Article 20)	
	Governors to report at least twice a year to the Diet (Article 54)	
Protecting secrets and setting salaries	Members cannot leak information, nor otherwise use information to their own advantage (Article 29)	Salaries of the Bank of Japan officials are decreased (political cost of independence).
	Standard for setting salaries to be developed (Article 31)	
Special loans (without collateral)	Ministry of Finance may request Bank of Japan to conduct business necessary to maintain an orderly financial system, including provision of loans (Article 38)	Special loans are clarified.
Vague description (Article 25)		
International businesses	Bank of Japan may buy and sell foreign exchange on its own account or as an agent of the government (Article 40)	Bank has power to intervene.

Table 4.2 (continued)

Old	New	Comments
On-site examination		
No description in the law	Bank of Japan may enter into a contract with financial institutions that become correspondents in business regarding on-site examination (Article 44)	On-site examination is clarified.
Bank notes		
Limit for issuance was set by the Diet	Bank of Japan can issue banknotes (Article 46)	No limit for issuance is given.
Bank of Japan budget		
Ministry of Finance approves the budget	Items that need approval by Ministry of Finance clarified; if budget not approved, reasons have to be given	This is an enhancement of independence.

Minister of Finance to dismiss executive directors, auditors, and advisers (Article 47) "whenever it is deemed particularly necessary for the attainment of the objective of the Bank."

The new Law changes this fundamental relationship between the Bank of Japan, Ministry of Finance, and government. The new Law states that "the Bank of Japan's autonomy regarding the currency and monetary control shall be respected (Article 3)" and more generally, "due consideration shall be given to the autonomy of the Bank's business operations." The power to remove Bank of Japan officers has been significantly limited to removal for incompetence, criminal behavior, or incapacity to discharge duties.

The stated autonomy, however, is constrained by three considerations in the new Law. First, in the same references to autonomy, the new law requires the Bank of Japan to "... always keep close contact with the government and exchange views sufficiently so that its currency and monetary control and the basic stance of the government's economic policy shall be mutually harmonious (Article 4)." This requirement, in practice, could mean anything from the mere exchange of views between the Bank of Japan and the government to a request from the government that monetary policy be compatible with other economic goals of government policy.

Second, the autonomy provision is not extended to the Bank's responsibility for financial stability or lender of last resort operations.

Third, the autonomy is not extended to foreign exchange market intervention in the new Law. Intervention remains primarily a responsibility of the Ministry of Finance. Domestic monetary policy and external considerations have conflicted on occasion. However, that was because domestic monetary policy was subject to pressures from the government. Now that domestic monetary policy is independent, exchange market intervention can be neutralized by sterilization. Theoretically sterilized intervention insulates domestic monetary policy during the exchange market intervention.

Process of Policy Formulation

The role of the Policy Board was reaffirmed in the 1998 Law. Even under the old Law, the Policy Board theoretically had significant decision-making power. Over time, however, the Policy Board failed to assume this power, and instead generally approved whatever the Bank staff through the Executive Board recommended. The Policy Board is reinstated with a different membership composition as the primary policy-making body of the Bank of Japan with respect to currency and monetary control issues. The Executive Board was abolished.

The newly reestablished Policy Board consists of nine members. There are three representatives of the Bank of Japan: the Bank's governor and two deputy governors. The majority, however, consists of six "Deliberative Members" selected by the Cabinet with the consent of the Diet among "experts on the economy of finance and academics (Article 23)."

The membership of the Policy Board differs significantly from the Policy Board established in 1949. First, the government has no formal representation on the Policy Bored, although representatives from the Ministry of Finance and the Economic Planning Agency can attend Board meetings to express views and even request a delay in a policy decision (Article 19). Second, the majority of members (six Deliberative Members) represent a broader viewpoint since they are to be chosen for their expertise rather than whether they represent a specific sector of the economy. In the 1942 Law the nongovernment representatives were required to represent financial institutions, agriculture, and commerce.

Transparency and Accountability

There was no meaningful requirement for transparency under the 1942 Law. The 1942 Law only specified that the Bank of Japan "shall make public a statement of the general condition of the operation of the Bank for each business period in accordance with the prescriptions of the competent Minister (Article 41)." This was interpreted to mean making statistical information available and providing special reports about the Bank of Japan's operations as well as providing an annual report. The new Law is a significant shift toward greater transparency in the formulation and execution of monetary policy.

Transparency is specified in five areas in the new Law. First, Article 3 states that in general the Bank of Japan is required to "clarify to the public the content of its decisions, as well as the process of decision making, regarding the currency and monetary control." Second, the minutes of each Policy Board meeting are to be distributed to the public after a certain period determined by the Board has expired (Article 20). Third, the Bank of Japan every six months is required to produce a documentation of the Policy Board's decisions through the Ministry of

Finance to the Diet and representatives of the Bank and the Policy Board are required to appear before the Diet on request (Article 54). The provision to pass reports through the Ministry of Finance is merely a formality and in this regard, the Ministry serves only as an agent since the Bank of Japan does not have a formal presence in the Diet. Fourth, disagreements between the Bank of Japan and the Ministry of Finance over the "current" expenditure budget are to be made public (Article 51). Current budget expenditures of the Bank of Japan are defined as those expenditures unrelated to the conduct of monetary operations. Fifth, the Bank of Japan executive and staff salary standards are to be publicly announced (Articles 31 and 32).

In practice, the public has already been given information[6] not only of decisions by the Policy Board but about their opinions and votes. In fact the candor of the discussions is notable. This alone is a significant enhancement of transparency in monetary policy decision making.

The 1942 Law made the Bank of Japan accountable to the Ministry of Finance, whereas the 1998 Law requires the Bank of Japan to be ultimately accountable to the Diet who in turn is responsible for appointing the nine members of the Policy Board.

Budgeting

The Bank of Japan's budget in the broadest sense was under the control of the Minister of Finance. The 1998 Law provides the Bank of Japan with enhanced autonomy in budget matters from determining salaries and promotions of its staff to preparing a budget that is not subject to a Ministry of Finance approval prior to submission to the Diet. Disagreements over the budget with the Ministry of Finance are to be made public, though the 1998 Law does not specify what steps will be taken to resolve the conflict.

Mikitani and Kuwayama (1998) have pointed out an unusual feature of the 1998 Law regarding budgeting issues. The new law requires the Bank of Japan to prepare a current expenditure budget with current expenditures to be determined by a government Cabinet order. This budget is required to be first submitted by the Ministry of Finance for approval with any disagreements to be made public. The problem is over how one will reasonably separate budget items into monetary and

---

6. Monetary policy reports are available on the Bank of Japan's Web site: *www. boj.org.jp*.

nonmonetary policy operations, and as a result the Ministry of Finance may retain de facto approval power over the entire Bank of Japan budget.

However, the fact remains that the Bank of Japan has received enhanced autonomy to determine its own budget and provided with a public forum to air disagreements with the Ministry of Finance, if any.

Special Uncollateralized Loans (Lender of Last Resort)

The 1942 Law implied the Ministry of Finance could direct the Bank of Japan to provide loans to any sector of the economy (Article 25). This was the basis used by he Ministry of Finance, for example, to provide Bank of Japan loans to Yamaichi Securities Company in 1965. The new Law does not significantly change this feature of the old Law, but only clarifies the situation. According to Article 38, "The Minister of Finance may request the Bank of Japan to conduct the business necessary to maintain the orderly financial system, including provision of loans, when it is believed to be especially necessary for the maintenance of the orderly financial system ...." The presumption is that the Bank of Japan may now refuse the request.

Thus the 1998 law assigns two responsibilities to the Bank of Japan: price stability and orderly financial markets. Bank of Japan autonomy, however, is explicitly given to price stability while initiative for orderly financial market intervention could come either from the Bank of Japan or the Minister of Finance. However, the decision and responsibility for lender of last resort now rests with the Bank of Japan. It remains to be seen whether the Bank of Japan could refuse a request from the Ministry of Finance or the Financial Supervisory Agency, if the request was made to prevent or limit systemic risk.

Exchange Rate Intervention

The Bank of Japan is permitted to conduct foreign exchange transactions on its own account, as an agent of the government, and as an agent of foreign central banks and international institutions (Article 40). The old Law was vague in this regard; for example, Article 23 of the old Law stated that the Bank of Japan "may, whenever deemed necessary, buy or sell foreign exchange." While more explicit, the new Law does not spell out a division of labor between the two agencies for exchange intervention, nor does it stress the Bank's autonomy in those transactions it conducts for its own account. The new Law essentially keeps the previous system in place in which the Ministry of Finance formulated and conducted exchange intervention operations through its own account.

On-site Examinations

The 1942 Law made no mention of on-site examinations while the new law is more explicit on the subject. In practice, the Ministry of Finance and the Bank of Japan alternated on-site examinations of banks; however, the Bank of Japan was concerned about its role in this process without an explicit legal basis. The Bank of Japan now has authority to conduct on-site examinations of those institutions for which it has provided, or is likely to provide loans, as part of its responsibility for orderly financial markets (Article 44). The results of these examinations are available to the Financial Supervision Agency on request.

The new law clarifies the ability of the Bank of Japan to conduct examinations on those institutions subject of lender of last resort operations.

Bank Notes

The old law limited the ability of the Bank of Japan to issue bank notes. The maximum was determined by the Cabinet and issuance in excess of the maximum required approval of the Minister of Finance. The 1998 Law removes the limit on bank note issuance, leaving that to be determined by the Bank of Japan. Technical issues such as the form of bank notes involve either the Cabinet or the Ministry of Finance.

Government Financing

The Bank of Japan may make uncollateralized loans to the government, subscribe or underwrite government bonds, and subscribe or underwrite Finance Bills (Article 34). This reaffirms provisions in the 1942 Law permitting the Bank of Japan to make uncollateralized loans and does not indicate whether the Bank of Japan has an independent choice in the matter other than that these loans are subject to limits set by the Diet.

Finance Bills are not in the same class as uncollateralized loans to the government. They are issued by the Ministry of Finance to bridge the short-term gap between receipts and expenditures. The problem was that they were issued at below market rates and were underwritten by the Bank of Japan. As a result, a considerable subsidy was provided to the Ministry of Finance. This was offset, however, by an equivalent deduction from the amount the Bank of Japan paid the government in profit at the end of the year.

The underwriting of Finance Bills, even though not a net subsidy to the Ministry of Finance, had been a subject of debate for over a decade as it has slowed the development of a wide and deep short-term government securities market in Japan. The practice of underwriting Finance Bills ended March 31, 1999. Finance Bills are now sold in the open market. There already exists a Treasury Bill market in Japan, but adding Finance Bills to the short-term government securities in the primary auction has deepened money and capital markets.

4.6   The New Bank of Japan Law and Measures of Central Bank Independence

There are clearly a number of significant changes in the 1998 Law compared to the 1942 Law. The old Law was the basis for widely referenced measures of Bank of Japan formal or legal independence. There is an issue as to whether measures or indexes of legal independence are an accurate projection of the actual legal parameters of the central bank and, more important, whether they are accurate measures of substantive or practical independence. Irrespective of this debate, however, it is instructive to apply the ranking methodology to incorporate the relevant features of the 1998 Law and to see how Japan's central bank independence rank index is changed.

The Cukierman, Webb, and Neyapti (1993) ranking methodology is employed for this task because it is the most detailed and transparent of the rankings provided in recent years. Their ranking for legal central bank independence is based on several types of information provided by the establishing legislation for each of the following four variables: chief executive office, policy formulation, objectives, and limitations on lending to the government. Each of the responses to each variable are weighted with each response given a numerical value. The numerical values combined with the assigned weights determine the overall legal central bank independence index value.

Table 4.3 presents the values assigned by Cukierman, Webb, and Neyapti (noted as CWN) to the Bank of Japan for the 1980 to 1989 period along with those assigned by the authors (noted as CHI) of this book based on the new Bank of Japan Law.

The computed index is 0.18 based on the old Law using the values assigned by Cukierman, Webb, and Neyapti to each attribute of legal independence in table 4.3. The index for the new Bank of Japan is 0.39 according to values assigned by the author's interpretation of the new Bank of Japan Law.[7] This raises Japan's ranking to the top third level of the rankings in table 4.1 using the Cukierman, Webb, and Neyapti rankings. The changes that increase the ranking relate to the terms of appointment of the chief operating officer, policy formulation, and objectives.

In terms of the appointment process, we have increased the value of item 1b because the Diet now plays a more important role than in the past. The value assigned to item 1c by Cukierman, Webb, and Neyapti of 0.83 is actually incorrect under the old Law. The old Law permitted dismissal for any reason and thus, the correct value would have been much lower; whereas, the new Law limits the ability of the chief officer to be dismissed. The value of 0.83 seems appropriate for the new Law. In terms of holding other offices (item 1d), the new Law neither permits nor prohibits holding other government offices, though it does prohibit holding a political position. Given that the position of governor is full time and given the language prohibiting political positions, we have interpreted the new Law as not permitting the simultaneous serving in another government ongoing appointment.

The policy formulation value was increased for items 2a and 2b. The Bank of Japan is now responsible for formulating policy with respect to price stability, and the Bank of Japan appears to have the final word on differences over how to pursue and define price stability.

The value for central bank objectives has been increased to reflect the role of price stability, although it is not the sole objective of the Bank of Japan, in the new Law. The score under item 3 should thus be raised from 0 to 0.6.

The increase in the index from 0.18 to 0.39 is meaningful, but it still understates the degree of price stability achieved by the Bank of Japan when considered in international perspective. A simple regression of the CPI inflation rate for selected countries over the 1975 to 1996 period against their central bank independence index will help illustrate the

---

7. Takahashi (1997) reached a similar result. He calculated the CWN index according to the new Bank of Japan Law and concluded that the index should be raised from 0.18 to 0.37.

Table 4.3
Revised central bank independence index for Bank of Japan based on 1998 Bank of Japan law

Item		Adjusted weight (2)	Japan's score CWN (3)	CHI (4)	Japan's weighted score CWN (2)×(3)	CHT (2)×(4)
1. Chief executive officer (CEO)						
a. Term of office (5 years)	0.05	0.05	0.5	0.5	0.025	0.025
b. Who appoints CEO? (executives collectively or executives and legislature)	0.05	0.05	0.25	0.75	0.0125	0.0375
c. Dismissal (for reasons not related to policy)	0.05	0.05	0.83	0.83	0.0415	0.0415
d. Can CEO hold other government offices? (with executive branch permission)	0.05	0.05	0.5	1.0	0.025	0.05
Subtotal					0.104	0.154
2. Policy formulation						
a. Who formulates monetary policy? (bank participates but has little influence, or bank alone)	0.05	0.05	0.67	1.0	0.0335	0.05
b. Who has final work in resolution of conflict? (executive branch has unconditional authority, or bank on issues clearly defined in the law as its objectives)	0.05	0.05	0	1.0	0	0.05
c. Role in government's budget process (central bank has no influence, or central bank active influence)	0.05	0.05	0	0	0	0
Subtotal					0.0335	0.10
3. Objectives						
a. Stated objectives do not include price stability						
b. Price stability is one goal, with the others compatible	0.15	0.15	0	0.6	0	0.09
c. Objectives include stable banking system						

4. Limitations on lending to government						
a. Advances for nonsecuritized lending (no legal limits)	0.15	0.1765	0	0		
b. Securitized lending (no legal limits)	0.1	0.1176	0	0		
c. Terms of lending (agreed between bank and executive)	0.1	0.1176	0.33	0.33	0.033	0.033
d. Potential borrowers from bank (not available)	0.05	NA				
e. Limits on central bank lending (not available)	0.025	NA				
f. Maturity of loans (no mention)	0.025	0.0294	0	0		
g. Interest rates on loans (no interest rate mentioned)	0.025	0.0294	0.25	0.25	0.006	0.066
h. Central bank prohibited from buying or selling government securities in the primary market?	0.025	0.0294	0	0		
Subtotal					0.039	0.039
Total = 1 + 2 + 3 + 4					0.18	0.39

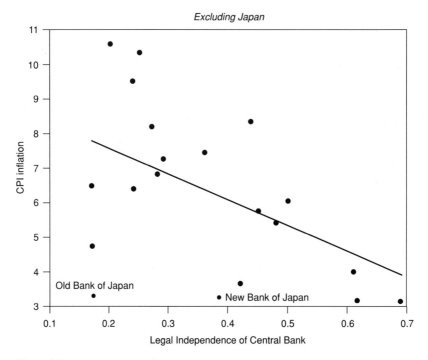

Figure 4.1
Central bank independence and inflation for 18 industrial countries (excluding Japan): 1975 to 1996. The actual inflation for each country is denoted by the scattered points and the predicted inflation for a given level of central bank independence by the fitted line.

difference between the old and new Bank of Japan. Figure 4.1 illustrates the actual and predicted inflation rates for a given level of central bank independence for 18 developed countries,[8] excluding Japan. The following regression is estimated:

CPI inflation rate = 9.10 − 7.54 ∗ Central bank index

$R^2 = 0.93$

As is typical with these types of regressions, the results indicate that there is a statistically significant (5 percent level of confidence) and negative relationship between a country's inflation rate and index of central bank independence. The actual and predicted inflation rates for the 18 countries are presented in figure 4.1. Japan's actual CPI infla-

---

8. The countries are Germany, Switzerland, Austria, Denmark, the United States, Canada, Ireland, the Netherlands, Australia, Sweden, Finland, the United Kingdom, Italy, New Zealand, France, Spain, Norway, and Belgium.

tion rate and central bank index (lower left-hand corner of figure 4.1) clearly indicate that Japan was not typical. Despite a low independence index, Japan's inflation rate of 3.31 percent was the lowest of the 19 industrial countries. Using the estimated regression and the old Law, Japan's index of 0.18 predicts an inflation rate of 7.74 percent over the 1975 to 1996 period compared to an actual average inflation rate of 3.31 percent. Japan's inflation performance, however, is still below what one would have predicted even using the new Bank of Japan index of 0.38. The new index value generates a predicted inflation rate of 6.16 percent, still almost twice as high as Japan's actual inflation rate.

The legal independence ranking of the Bank of Japan increased significantly as a result of the 1998 Bank of Japan Law. However, these indexes only measure legal independence. There may be a significant difference between practical and legal independence. The Bank of Japan during the two decades prior to the 1998 revision is a clear example of this difference. Starting in the mid-1970s, the Bank of Japan secured meaningful practical independence (Cargill, Hutchison, and Ito 1997) but lacked the legal basis because it continued to operate under the 1942 Law. The new Bank of Japan now has the legal basis to function in an independent manner.

4.7   Concluding Comments

The Bank of Japan Law has been the operating basis of monetary policy in Japan since 1882. There is little difference between the first version in 1882 and the wartime 1942 Law that remained in force until March 31, 1998. The Bank of Japan Law defined a relationship between the central bank and the government that rendered the Bank of Japan legally dependent on the Ministry of Finance. While much of the conduct of monetary policy in Japan through the early 1970s was consistent with the Bank of Japan Law, monetary policy began to reflect a degree of independence and flexibility in practice after the mid-1970s.

Efforts to measure the independence of the degree of central bank independence in Japan have for the most part concluded that the Bank of Japan is among the world's most dependent central banks. This has generated a "Japan puzzle" for studies that argue that there existed a statistically strong relationship between central bank independence and inflation performance. Japan throughout much of the postwar period has had an impressive record of price stability, especially during the 1975 to 1990 period. The conditions that permitted the Bank of

Japan to function as a price stabilizing dependent central bank, however, began to change in the early 1990s.

The revision of the Bank of Japan Law in 1998 was the outcome of a number of forces. Renewed interest in central bank institutional design to enable central banks to better pursue price stability and financial liberalization provided the background for institutional redesign in Japan. Depressed economic conditions and financial distress in Japan provided an additional incentive to consider revision of the 1942 Law. The decline in the reputation and credibility of the Ministry of Finance is especially important because it provided the political conditions that made possible the independence of the Bank of Japan.

The 1998 revision had little to do with dissatisfaction over past monetary policy, although some observes such as Ueda (2000) imply that the bubble economy would have been less likely had the Bank of Japan been independent of the Ministry of Finance. Irrespective of one's view of Ueda's argument, the Bank of Japan also lost reputation. Many blamed the Bank of Japan for the asset inflation, then blamed the Bank of Japan for waiting so long before bursting the bubble. Some argue the Bank of Japan shares part of the responsibility with the Ministry of Finance in dealing with nonperforming loan problems in the early to mid-1990s, since both alternated on-site examinations. Nonetheless, the Ministry of Finance was the primary financial regulatory authority during this critical period. The loss of reputation by the Ministry of Finance was much larger than the loss of reputation by the Bank of Japan. The Bank of Japan as an institution, however, did lose credibility in 1998 as inappropriate conduct of a staff member was revealed to have taken place in the Banking Bureau. This was an unfortunate event that resulted in the resignation of the governor and deputy governor in March 1998.

Thus the new Bank of Japan was not primarily the outcome of failed monetary policy. The new Bank of Japan reflects a long overdue recognition of the need to change the legal basis of Japan's central bank. In a sense, the legal structure caught up with the de facto independence enjoyed by the Bank of Japan since the mid-1970s. The new Bank of Japan reflects the general consensus that formally independent central banks are more likely to generate better policy outcomes and a recognition, although not publicly expressed, that the underlying conditions that assisted the Bank of Japan's price stabilization policies in the past were no longer present. In the context of the Big Bang reforms, Japan would have been seriously remiss if she had not revised the legal basis of the Bank of Japan.

5

Inflation Targeting,
Liquidity Traps, and the
New Bank of Japan

5.1   Introduction

The economic and financial condition of the Japanese economy at the beginning of the new century is precarious, posing a particularly difficult environment for the Bank of Japan as it adapted to the new institutional arrangements associated with the Bank of Japan Law revision that became effective in April 1998. Sluggish growth and recession characterized the Japanese economy after 1992. The contraction of real output at the end of 1997 and through 1998, that is, five quarters in a row, had not occurred since 1950. The CPI inflation rate averaged less than 1 percent from 1994 to 1999,[1] (figure 2.2). Interbank interest rates declined to just above zero in tandem with the drop in the discount rate to 0.5 percent in the fall of 1995, a postwar low, reflecting the weak real sector and an attempt at monetary stimulation. By mid-1999, the overnight rate stood at 0.01 percent, the 2-year government bond rate at 0.48 percent, the corporate bond rate at 0.80 percent and the 10-year government bond rate at 1.67 percent.

A central question is whether a central bank in these circumstances can do more to stop deflation and restore growth to the economy. With interest rates at historic lows and base money growing, what other policies might have proved more effective to move Japan out of its slump? The situation at the end of the 1990s was reminiscent of the early 1930s in many countries during which monetary policy seemed powerless to provide effective stimulus in the context of falling output and interest rates near zero. This situation is frequently termed a

---

1. The low positive CPI-inflation rate is also in reality "deflation," because of the well-known upward biases in the CPI index (Boskin et al. 1997). Studies conducted by the Bank of Japan suggest the magnitude of bias in the Japan-CPI index is around 1 percent (Shiratsuka 1999).

"liquidity trap," although this characterization and its applicability to Japan are controversial.

Given these deflationary conditions, some analysts have argued that adoption of a credible inflation target by the Bank of Japan would have helped take the economy out of recession sooner (e.g., Krugman 1998, 1999; Cargill, Hutchison, and Ito 1999; Ito 1999; Posen 1998, 1999). This policy, however, would be against a background of other significant institutional changes affecting the Bank of Japan and during a period of severe financial sector distress. The 1998 Bank of Japan Law represents the most important change in the institutional structure and legal status of the central bank since its formation in 1882. This represents a substantial increase in the Bank of Japan's institutional independence from other parts of government, as discussed in chapter 4. Moreover implementation and enforcement of new regulatory and supervisory policies, as well as reshuffling of these responsibilities among the Bank of Japan, the Ministry of Finance and the new Financial Supervisory Agency and Financial Reconstruction Commission, represents a new direction in this area for Japan as discussed in chapter 3.

Although this is a period of transition for Japan, one may look to institutional reforms and policy changes at other central banks around the world to see how they influence monetary and stabilization policy responsibilities and facilitate the lender-of-last-resort, regulatory, and supervisory roles. This chapter focuses on central bank institutional and policy reform and macroeconomic policy issues in the international context, especially as it relates to price stabilization. In this context, we consider the effects of increased institutional independence on the operations of central banks and how inflation targeting might be useful during episodes of deflation and recession as well as a framework to prevent inflation. To address this issue in the Japanese context, however, we first consider alternative explanations for the decline in output and prices other than a "liquidity trap." Alternative explanations focus on the "credit crunch," banking, and nonperforming loan problems that characterized Japan's economy in the 1990s, especially in 1998 and 1999. To shed light on how an inflation-targeting regime might work in Japan, we then turn to recent experiences in other countries, focusing in particular on New Zealand. To better understand the context of introducing an inflation-targeting regime in a deflationary environment—the opposite of recent central bank reforms around the world—we consider the Swedish experience in the 1930s as well as Japan's experience in the 1930s.

5.2   Liquidity Trap, Credit Crunch, and Banking Malaise

Japan is the first major industrial economy to face serious deflation since the Great Depression of the 1930s. Fears of a liquidity trap emerged along with interest rates hovering above a zero interest rate floor. A liquidity trap, in its simplest textbook form, is characterized by a very low level of the nominal interest rate (a minimum point, perhaps zero) and the expectation of a future interest rate increase (bond price decline). Rather than accept capital losses with the anticipated fall in bond prices, increases in the money supply do not induce a rise in the demand for bonds or a rise in spending. In this case the demand for money is infinitely elastic at this point. The central bank is powerless to stimulate the economy as spending is not induced by a rise in money balances, and interest rates can not be further lowered.

Liquidity Trap Argument

Was Japan in a liquidity trap at the end of the 1990s? The most visible proponent of this view is Krugman (1998, 1999). He forcefully argued that Japan was in a liquidity trap and recommended that the Bank of Japan bring inflation and inflationary expectations up to 4 percent and keep it there for 15 years. Focusing less on a potential liquidity trap, and more on the need to introduce a stabilizing and credible monetary expansion, more modest proposals were also suggested. Posen (1998), for example, recommended that the Bank of Japan adopt a 3 percent target for 2000 and a 2 percent target over the longer term. Cargill, Hutchison, and Ito (1999) and Ito (1999) also suggested an inflation target of around 1 to 3 percent.

Krugman made the standard liquidity trap argument, extended to focus on intertemporal aspects, rational agents, optimization, and models with rigid and flexible prices. But the key element of his analysis, emphasized in its simplest terms, is that the equilibrium real interest rate is negative in a liquidity trap. Given a nominal interest rate floor of zero, Krugman argued that positive expected inflation is necessary to generate negative real interest rates and achieve a level of aggregate demand to restore full employment.[2]

---

2. Krugman (1998) states: "[t]he problem is ... that the full-employment real interest rate is negative. And monetary policy therefore cannot get the economy to full employment unless the central bank can convince the public that the future inflation rate will be sufficiently high to permit the negative real interest rate. That's all there is to it."

Two pieces of empirical evidence were employed by Krugman to support the liquidity trap argument. First, he pointed to the fact that short-term interest rates reached a minimum point in 1999, virtually zero as illustrated in figure 2.4. The official discount rate was lowered to 1.0 percent in April 1995 and to 0.5 percent in September 1995. The target interbank rate was lowered from 0.45 percent to 0.25 percent in September 1998 and, by mid-1999, was lowered to just above zero. The record low discount rate was maintained for three years and the economy had moved further into recession. The yield curve was virtually flat, as the 10-year government bond yield (figure 2.4) declined to less than 1 percent in September 1998, before rising to 2.0 percent in early 1999 and falling off to 1.7 percent by July 1999. The low interest rates seen in Japan at the end of the 1990s were unprecedented for any industrial country since the 1930s.

Second, Krugman pointed out that injections of liquidity by the central bank had not been very effective in raising the growth rate of the broader money aggregates. The monetary base grew 25 percent from 1994 to 1997, but the broader monetary aggregate (M2 + CDs) grew only 11 percent and bank credit not at all. More recent statistics indicated that "money hoarding" continued to be evident in 1998, as an expansion of the monetary base in the range of 8 to 10 percent resulted in only about a 3.5 percent growth in M2 + CDs (figures 5.1 and 5.2). In 1999 the monetary base growth rate declined to the 4 to 6 percent range without any discernable effect on the money supply. Bank lending collapsed in early 1998, as shown in figure 2.5. Moreover, at least through the end of 1998, low interest rates and expansion in the monetary base had not helped increase aggregate demand as the economy continued in a deep recession.

Alternative Explanations: Fiscal Policy, Banking Problems, and a Credit Crunch

The picture of Japan in the 1990s, however, was not as simple as Krugman suggests. The Japanese economy began a fledging recovery in 1996 in terms of real GDP growth illustrated in figure 2.1, and then fell back into recession in late 1997. The immediate cause of the sharp downturn in 1997 appears to be associated with an increase in the consumption tax rate, from 3 percent to 5 percent, combined with an end to a temporary income tax cut in April 1997. This amounted to a tax increase of 9 trillion yen or 1.8 percent of 1997 GDP.

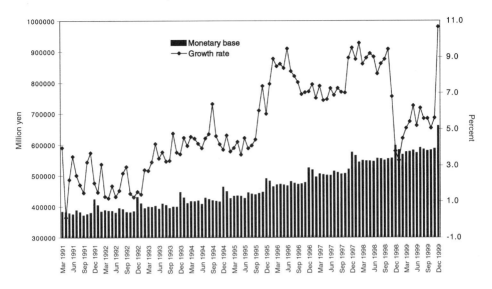

Figure 5.1
Monetary base, level and growth rate: March 1991 to December 1999. Annual growth rate calculated from the same quarter in the previous year to the current quarter. Source: Bank of Japan (*www.boj.or.jp*).

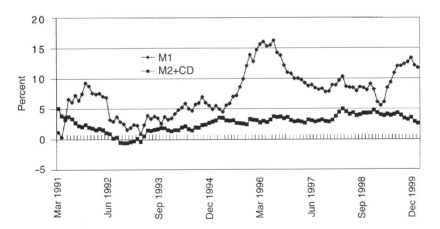

Figure 5.2
Money supply growth rate: March 1991 to December 1999. Annual growth rate calculated from the same quarter in the previous year to the current quarter. Source: Bank of Japan (*www.boj.or.jp*).

Fiscal contraction was compounded by a credit crunch caused by massive nonperforming loans accumulating in the financial system. Banks were under pressure to increase their risk-adjusted capital ratio. Less than candid reporting by both banks and the Ministry of Finance about the magnitude of the nonperforming loan problem made it difficult for banks to raise capital in domestic and international financial markets. Banks were thus forced to respond by a sharp contraction in bank lending and hence, generate a "credit crunch" in Japan.

The capital-asset ratio of the 20 largest financial institutions in Japan had fallen significantly between 1994 and the end of 1998. Amid market, government, and international pressure (Bank for International Settlements capital adequacy standards), Japanese financial institutions attempted to raise capital ratios. They responded by reducing asset accumulation, namely lowering the amount of loans outstanding. Building capital-asset ratios by restraining lending takes a long period of time, however, and induces a credit squeeze in the process.

The sharp decline in lending may also be attributable to a more cautious lending attitude by Japanese banks given their recent experience with the buildup of nonperforming loans and, with the deepening recession, weakening of firm balance sheets and rise in bankruptcies. Figures 5.3 and 5.4 show the number of bankruptcies and the total liabilities to banks associated with the bankruptcies. The all-time high of 3.1 trillion yen in liabilities associated with bankruptcies was recorded in the month of March 1999, but the trend line shows a sustained rise to the highest point in the postwar period towards the end of the decade.

It is noteworthy that the actual number of firm bankruptcies was higher in the mid-1980s, but in the 1990s, large firms with large outstanding loans suspended payments to banks unlike previous periods. These circumstances make firms less desirable potential borrowers than had previously been the case from the banks' point of view. But it also had the self-reinforcing effect of tightening credit conditions and worsening the recession.

Evidence of a credit crunch is also suggested by the Bank of Japan *Tankan*-Short-Term Economic Survey of Enterprises and two related surveys conducted by the Japan Finance Corporation for Small Business and the People's Finance Corporation,[3] shown in Figure 5.5.

---

3. These two institutions are government banks and are part of an extensive system of government or public financial intermediation referred to as the Fiscal Investment and Loan Program administered by the Ministry of Finance (Cargill and Yoshino 2000).

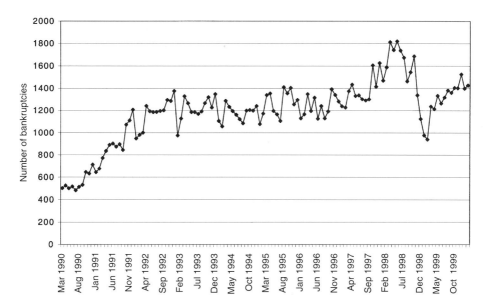

Figure 5.3
Corporate bankruptcies, number of cases: March 1990 to December 1999. Tokyo Shoko
Research (*www.tsr-net.co.jp*).

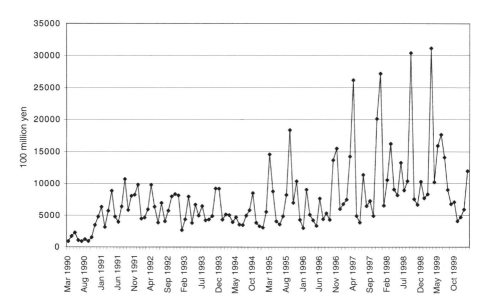

Figure 5.4
Corporate bankruptcies, gross liabilities (100 million yen): March 1990 to December 1999.
Source: Tokyo Shoko Research (*www.tsr-net.co.jp*).

(1) *Tankan* - Short-Term Economic Survey of Enterprises in Japan (December, 1999)

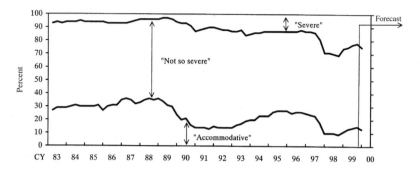

(2) Monthly Survey on Trends of Small Businesses (Mid-February, 2000)

(3) Quarterly Survey of Small Businesses in Japan (Mid-December, 1999)

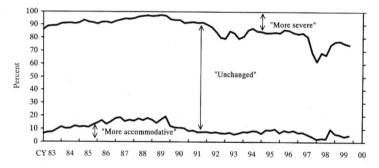

Figure 5.5
Lending attitude of financial institutions as perceived by enterprises. Severe means that
enterprises perceive that financial institutions are reluctant to lend while accommodative
means that enterprises perceive that financial institutions are willing to satisfy their
credit requests. Source: Bank of Japan (2000).

This surveys asks firms their views of the "lending attitude of financial institutions," and distinguishes between principal enterprises and small enterprises. Despite the low interest rate environment, the *Tankan* survey indicates a sharp tightening of credit conditions in Japan from mid-1997 through 1998 facing both principal and small enterprises. The "lending attitudes" of financial institutions, at least from the perspective of borrowers, was more stringent in 1998 compared to the mid-1990s. Attitudes, however, improved somewhat in 1999.

A credit crunch implies that injections of liquidity (base and narrow money expansion) do not increase credit and aggregate lending, despite the existence of demand for bank loans by corporations at the prevailing interest rate. The existence of credit crunch may be explained as a disequilibrium phenomenon, or a problem arising from asymmetric information problems. This is exactly what occurred in Japan. Base and narrow money increased at a robust pace in 1997 to 1999, but the broader money aggregates most directly related to spending in the economy grew modestly. Most disturbing is that aggregate lending by banks decreased sharply, reflecting the tightening of credit conditions faced by enterprises in Japan.

Beyond these quantifiable factors, domestic and international confidence in the Japanese banking system also appears to have been adversely affected by the general malaise hanging over the economy. Several identifiable factors contributed to this malaise. The emergence of the "Japan premium" representing the additional basis points charged on international loans to Japanese banks that are viewed as risky played a role. Figure 2.9 shows the premium Japanese banks paid in the Eurodollar market. The premium is calculated as the difference between the quoted rates of TIBOR (in the Tokyo offshore market where most banks are Japanese) and LIBOR (in the London offshore market where most sampled banks are western). The Japan premium is the extra expense Japanese banks must pay for raising funds in overseas markets. The downgrading of the investment-grade ratings (by international credit-rating agencies such as Moody's) on debt issued by Japanese financial institutions and, later, by the Japanese government was also a contributing factor. More generally, the negative publicity over the Japanese financial system and economy clearly contributed to a very pessimistic atmosphere in Japan in the late 1990s.

Confluence of Events

The liquidity trap explanation has merit, but the other explanations—fiscal contraction, nonperforming loans, credit crunch, and confidence shock—also seem plausible. Low interest rates, slow broad money growth, falling commercial loans, and robust base money growth are consistent with either a liquidity trap or the credit crunch explanation. The credit crunch story emphasizes the supply of credit constraint, which is supported by the *Tankan* and related survey results and evidence of a Japan premium for banks.

Krugman dismisses the credit crunch argument, however, arguing that banks with a large portfolio of nonperforming loans should take on excessive risk and stand ready to lend to even questionable borrowers. Excessive lending rather than a credit contraction would be predicted as banks gamble on high-risk projects, hoping to restore solvency before they are forced into bankruptcy by the financial authorities.

This type of excessive lending occurred in Japan at the early stages of the banking crisis. *Jusen* (real estate lending financial institutions) lending actually grew rapidly in 1991 and 1992 as they faced growing problems with nonperforming loans. But at this stage of the banking problem and the government shift to the new financial supervision and regulatory regime discussed in chapter 3, the supervisory authorities are not sitting idly by and allowing excessive risk-taking on the part of banks. The new Bank of Japan discussed in chapter 4 is also contributing to the pressure placed on private banks to be more transparent and improve their balance sheets. Greater stringency in banking oversight is the new modus operandi in Japan since 1998.

To address this problem, many banks in Japan in 1999 were recapitalized with public funds. The March 1999 capital injection was mainly in the form of preferred convertible stock, which provides the government with considerable influence over how the bank utilizes the capital injection. In principle, this should eventually ease the credit squeeze and induce banks, particularly with further injections of liquidity into the banking system, to increase lending.

On balance, there were probably some elements of the liquidity trap and a credit crunch and nonperforming loan explanation behind the extremely weak economic performance of Japan in the second half of the 1990s. However, it is doubtful that generating expectations of a 4 percent or greater inflation rate over a 15-year period is really necessary to resolve the problem. Although Krugman dismisses fiscal stimulus as a solution, primarily on Ricardian equivalence grounds, there is some recent evidence that the large fiscal injections in 1998 and 1999 combined with the injection of capital into the banking system were beginning to take effect. The GDP growth rate jumped in the first quarter of 1999 by almost 6 percent annualized. This large fiscal stimulus in 1998 is generally regarded as an important cause of the turn around in the first quarter of 1999, and many observes argue that further fiscal stimulus is required in the form of tax reduction rather than spending. Indeed, Posen (1998) argued that the announced fiscal stimulus measures in the 1990s were effectively much smaller than claimed by the Ministry of Finance and that when serious fiscal stimulus was tried, the economy responded in the anticipated manner. He argued that a sufficiently large fiscal expansion would have worked to end economic stagnation and deflation.

5.3 Inflation Targeting and Central Bank Reform

Even if one does not believe that Japan was in a liquidity trap situation at the end of the 1990s, there still might be merit to having some form of inflation or price-level targeting. A number of countries have introduced this form of policy, usually in tandem with broader measures of central bank reform.

The Theory of Inflation Targeting and Central Bank Independence

In the past decade more than twenty-five countries in different parts of the world have instituted central bank reforms giving their central banks more independence from other parts of government. This trend is particularly impressive since changes in central bank legislation were comparatively rare in the first four decades of the postwar period (Cukierman 1996). The 1998 Bank of Japan Law change now places Japan in the group of country's granting their central banks substantially greater institutional independence.

The main motivating factor in most central bank reforms has been the quest for greater price stability against a background of persistent inflation, and hope that giving central banks greater institutional independence will help to achieve this objective. The problem of persistent inflation, has characterized most industrial countries over the past half century. In this respect, the background for the Bank of Japan Law

reform seems oddly out of place since Japan has had the lowest inflation rate among the major industrial countries in the 1980s and 1990s.

Walsh (1995a) and Persson and Tabellini (1993) make a case for
designing "contracts" for central banks, providing them with incentives to maintain long-term price stability while providing some leeway for short-run output stabilization. Walsh demonstrates that, when
the central bankers care about their own compensation and social
welfare, the optimal contract design would make their compensation
depend only on the realized rate of inflation. He shows that this compensation structure may resemble an inflation-targeting rule in that the
central banker would be rewarded according to how close to target
actual inflation turned out. That is, the "transfer function" (compensation to the central banker) would be a simple linear function of the
realized rate of inflation and this would be sufficient to eliminate inflationary bias in the context of the Barro-Gordon model (1983).

Recent work in this area has extended the basic Walsh model (see
Walsh 1998 for a comprehensive review). Work by Svensson (1997a,
1997b), for example, shows how the linear inflation contract is affected
when the inflation bias is time dependent because of persistence in the
unemployment process. The simple linear Walsh-contract is no longer
optimal in this case, but a state-contingent contract can support the
optimal commitment policy.

The work by Walsh and others link the incentive structure of the central bank (compensation and other rewards) to inflation, and hence
suggests that a form of "inflation targeting" will be followed. One may
interpret the contracting approach as providing an incentive framework within the institutional structure of the (independent) central
bank. The inflation-targeting regime is not dictated by the government
but rather is induced by the incentive structure. It is important to note,
however, that this is not a strict inflation-targeting regime in the traditional sense, since the central banker, caring about society's welfare as
well as his/her own compensation, will respond appropriately to supply shocks with an activist policy to stabilize output. Hence short-run
inflation will not be constant, but this is due to stabilization policy
responding to unexpected shocks and not to the central bank generating inflation by attempting to take advantage of pre-determined
inflationary expectations. Indeed, expected inflation in this context is
constant and equal to society's optimal rate of inflation that holds on
average. Hence inflation bias is eliminated.

Inflation targeting is often introduced in the context of legislative action, so it may not provide greater formal institutional independence. It does provide the central bank with a clear objective (a targeted rate of inflation), however, and frequently allows substantial freedom in how policy is conducted in order to meet that objective. Hence, although the central bank is typically presented with a mandated inflation target (goal dependence), it has some leeway in how it achieves the objective (instrument independence).[4] Other important issues also arise in the actual implementation of an inflation-targeting regime: design and measurement of the inflation target, transparency and flexibility of the policy (legitimate escape clauses), and the time frame in which the target is to be met.

Central Bank Reforms

Central bank institutional reform has been prompted by the new theoretical developments and by empirical evidence linking the independence of central banks to good inflation performance. The impressive performance of some highly independent central banks such as the German Bundesbank (prior to the start of the European Monetary Union in 1999) and the Swiss National Bank has influenced the debate. The German Bundesbank, prior to giving up policy discretion to the European Central Bank, had been an especially influential model of monetary stability. The Bundesbank served as an anchor for the rest of the European Union member states. They usually tied policy to Germany and attempted to "import" credibility for announced low-inflation objectives. The European Central Bank was in large part designed to ensure the same degree of legal and operational independence the Bundesbank had achieved.

Legal independence is often made possible by changes in central banking laws and other legislation involving the relationship of the central bank to other parts of the government. Indeed, many of these reforms involved completely rewriting existing central bank charters. Among the industrial countries in this group are Belgium, France, Italy, Portugal, Spain, New Zealand, the United Kingdom, and, in 1998, Japan. The European countries listed, excepting the United Kingdom, made the legislative changes so as to conform to the Maastricht

---

4. See Debelle and Fischer (1994) for the distinction between goal and instrument independence.

Treaty's convergence criteria requiring that central bank must be made legally independent as an entry condition into European Monetary Union. In contrast, the United Kingdom, New Zealand, and Japan undertook these changes without being pressured from external sources to do so. Rather, the motivating factors were due to domestic political and economic considerations.

A number of developing, transition, and newly industrial economies have also followed the trend. Some of the developing economies in this group include Argentina, Chile, Colombia, Mexico, Venezuela, and Pakistan. Most of the countries in the former Soviet Union, and others in formerly socialist Eastern Europe, have also undertaken significant central banking reform (Maxfield 1997). In terms of newly industrial countries, South Korea presents an interesting case where greater legal independence for the central bank was extended in the midst of economic crisis and was part of a series of reform measures agreed upon by a newly elected government and the International Monetary Fund (Cargill 1998a, 1998b).

International Evidence on Inflation Targeting

An element in many central bank reforms is some form of inflation targeting. Although these reforms have been introduced as a means to control inflation, inflation targeting may, in principle, work to offset deflationary pressures such as those faced by Japan at the end of the 1990s.

Inflation-targeting regimes sometimes have been introduced as an integral part of institutional reform granting the central bank greater independence. New Zealand is the most clear-cut case of this type of reform.[5] Spain's inflation targeting regime was also directly a consequence of, and in compliance with, the new law granting greater autonomy to the Bank of Spain. The Bank of Korea Act, revised in December 1997, mandates price stability as the sole objective of monetary policy in the context of an inflation target set in consultation with the government. In other cases, however, the central bank has intro-

---

5. This seems logical from the point of view of the government. There is little reason for a government desiring control over the central bank, and favoring discretionary policy actions, to support inflation targets. However, once a central bank is provided with a greater degree of independence from direct government action, adoption of inflation targets limits discretionary action, imposes "goal dependence" on the central bank, and usually provides a high degree of transparency in policy.

duced the reforms on its own initiative. Sometimes this has followed significant changes in the institutional and legal independence of the central bank (e.g., United Kingdom), but not always. Sweden, for example, introduced inflation targeting following its departure from a fixed exchange rate regime, but initially there was no corresponding new central bank legislation. In Australia, the decision to target inflation was a unilateral decision by the central bank unrelated to other reforms.

At least ten countries adopted some form of inflation targeting in the 1990s: New Zealand, Canada, the United Kingdom, Sweden, Finland, Australia, Spain, Israel, Chile, and South Korea. These countries are covered in the table 5.1, adapted from Kahn and Parrish (1998).[6] The table provides information on a number of features and technical aspects of these inflation-targeting regimes. This information includes the dates inflation targets were first issued, the target ranges in force in mid-1998, the target period (time frame), the measure of inflation employed in the targeting procedure, the way targets are announced, aspects of publicly released inflation reports, and whether the inflation forecasts are published.

New Zealand[7]

New Zealand became the first country to introduce inflation targets formally when Parliament passed the Reserve Bank of New Zealand Act of 1989, effective from February 1990. In many respects New Zealand's experience has been a showcase for a number of other countries adopting or considering adopting some form of inflation targeting and could also be a model for Japan.

The Reserve Bank of New Zealand (RBNZ) is given considerable independence from political influence in the way it pursues the inflation target (instrument independence). The inflation target was established as the single formal objective of monetary policy, and the specific target range is formally subject to negotiation and mutual agreement between the government and the central bank (goal codependence). Further the Reserve Bank, and the Governor in particular, is held accountable for achieving this objective.

---

6. Recent international comparisons of inflation targeting experiences are provided by Mishkin and Posen (1997), Bernanke et al. (1999), Kahn and Parrish (1998), and Debelle (1997). A number of in-depth case studies have also investigated individual country experiences of inflation targeting; for example, see Hutchison and Walsh (1998a, 1998b) for New Zealand and Baumgartner et al. (1997) for Sweden.

7. This section draws on Hutchison and Walsh (1998a).

Table 5.1
Summary of inflation targeting frameworks

	New Zealand	Canada	United Kingdom	Sweden	Finland	Australia	Spain	Israel[a]	Chile[a]
Date first issued	March 1990	February 1991	October 1992	January 1993	February 1993	Approx. April 1993[b]	Summer 1994[b]	December 1991[c]	Approx. 1990[d]
Current target	0–3%	1–3% with "midpoint" 2%	2.5%	2 ± 1%	2%	2–3% ("thick point")	Less than 3%	7–10%	4.5%
Time frame	5 years (to 2003)	through end 2001	1997 onward	1995 onward	1996 onward	On average over the cycle	By late 1997, less than 2% thereafter	1 year	1 year
Inflation measure	CPIX (CPI excluding credit services)	CPI (Underlying inflation used operationally)	RPIX (retail price index excluding mortgage interest payments)	CPI	Underlying CPI	Underlying CPI	CPI	CPI	CPI
Target announcement	Defined in Policy Target Agreement (PTA) between the Minister of Finance and the governor of the central bank	Joint agreement between the Minister of Finance and the governor of the central bank	Chancellor of the Exchequer	Governing Board of the Bank of Sweden (Sveriges Riksbank), which is an authority of the parliament	Bank of Finland	Reserve Bank of Australia	Bank of Spain	Minister of Finance in consultation with the Prime Minister and the governor of the central bank	Central Bank of Chile

Inflation report	Since March 1990. Quarterly today, formerly semi-annually	Semi-annual since May 1995	Quarterly since February 1993	Since October 1993. Quarterly today, formerly three times per year	No	Semi-annual since May 1997	Semi-annual since March 1995	Since March 1998	Annual, every September
Inflation forecasts published?	Yes	No	Yes	Yes	No	No	No	No	No

Sources: Debelle; Bernanke, Laubach, Mishkin, and Posen; Reserve Bank of New Zealand's Policy Targets Agreement (December 1997); Bank of Canada (May 1998); Bank of England (August 1997); Sveriges Riksbank (June 1998); Bank of Israel; and Banco Central de Chile.

a. Israel and Chile also target the exchange rate.

b. The Reserve Bank of Australia dates the introduction of inflation targets to approximately April 1993 and the Bank of Spain to summer 1994. However, Bernanke, Laubach, Mishkin, and Posen argue that Australia did not introduce targets until September 1994 and Spain until November 1994.

c. *Financial Times*, December 18, 1990.

d. Since 1990 the Central Bank of Chile has been required by law to announce each September an inflation rate to be reached the following year. By the mid-1990s these "targets" had gained credibility.

The Act was introduced both as a means to help reinforce the process of lowering the inflation rate, already underway for several years prior to its introduction, as well as to gain credibility for a stated policy of sustained low inflation. In New Zealand the inflation target was introduced when inflation was around 7 percent, having already fallen from around 16 percent. The New Zealand experience has attracted much academic and policy attention (e.g., Debelle and Fischer 1994; Hutchison 1995a; McCallum 1996; Walsh 1995b), partly because disinflation in New Zealand was quite successful: average inflation declined from 11.3 percent in 1985 to 1989, to 3.3 percent in 1990 to 1992, and to 2.3 percent in 1993 to 1996. A great deal of attention has also focused on the formal institutional arrangement introduced in New Zealand both for setting and implementing inflation targets and for ensuring the RBNZ is held accountable for achieving the targets.

The RBNZ Act still allows some discretion in monetary policy. As Walsh (1995b) argues, it may have some features of an "optimal" contract for central bankers, but there is still room to renegotiate. This process of renegotiating the Policy Targets Agreement (PTA) has allowed politicians to intervene and influence policy at crucial times. In particular, New Zealand has experienced two recessions since the Act was implemented and both times the PTA was renegotiated to allow some easing of policy.

Hutchison and Walsh (1998a) show, however, that the low cost of renegotiating the PTA could be a problem for the credibility of the central bank's commitment to low inflation. Equally important is that the PTA seems to have been eroded along other dimensions—particularly by the subtle change in the objective function of the RBNZ. Raising the cost of renegotiating the PTA may have some merit. Of course, since the Parliament created the Reserve Bank Act of 1989 and the new monetary regime, it could also change the underlying Bank law even if the costs of renegotiating the PTA were substantial.

Although the new monetary regime in New Zealand points to certain limitations, average inflation has been low by historical and international norms since the central bank reform. The focus on inflation and continuous and clear communication of the Bank's objectives and views on policy have greatly enhanced the accountability and transparency of monetary policy in New Zealand. Accountability and transparency—mandated by various provisions of the 1989 Act—may in turn have contributed to public support of policies set to achieve a low rate of inflation.

Other Inflation Targeting Experiences

New Zealand's experience highlights a number of key features that seem to have contributed to their successful inflation-targeting regime. A clearly defined inflation target as the single objective of policy, with the governor of the central bank taking sole responsibility for achieving this objective, is central. The reliance on forecasts of inflation in aiming at the target and the use of inflation reports to communicate clearly, and in a transparent manner, the goals and constraints on policy have also played a role. Finally, allowing some flexibility in the implementation of policy, particularly when adverse economic conditions arise, seems to have helped stabilize the economy and had the added benefit of maintaining political support for the inflation-targeting regime.

The other countries adopting inflation targeting share many of these key features. All of the countries explicitly target inflation rates below 3 percent, excepting Chile and Israel, which began at much higher inflation rates initially. Many have an explicit time frame during which the targeted inflation rate is in force (New Zealand, Canada, Israel, and Chile), while others have an indefinite period (United Kingdom, Sweden, Finland, and Spain). The inflation measure employed in most countries (eight of the nine) is some form of the CPI, frequently adjusted to better measure "underlying" inflation (New Zealand, Canada, Finland, and Australia).

In addition to New Zealand, central banks in several countries determine and announce targets jointly with the Minister of Finance or related government entity (Canada and Israel). In some cases, the government sets, directly or indirectly, the inflation target for the central bank (United Kingdom and Sweden), while in other cases the central bank alone announces the target (Finland, Australia, Spain, and Chile). Like New Zealand, most central banks targeting inflation issue regular inflation reports. But only the central banks of New Zealand, the United Kingdom, and Sweden regularly publish inflation forecasts.

What Has Inflation Targeting Accomplished?

There is some question as to how much the adoption of inflation targeting regimes have really changed the short-term operation of monetary policy and contributed to lower inflation rates. Kahn and Parrish (1998), in their review of inflation targeting experiences and evidence from policy "reaction" functions, find mixed evidence as to whether significant changes in operating procedures have actually occurred. They raise the possibility that numerical inflation targets may simply formalize a monetary policy strategy that is already implicitly in place. Representatives from the Federal Reserve System have also questioned the value of changing to an inflation-targeting regime when they have already achieved and maintained a low rate of inflation.

Hutchison (1995a) and Hutchison and Walsh (1998b), considering only the case of New Zealand, question whether the introduction of inflation targeting, or simply a large and long-lasting recession, was mainly responsible for that country's successful disinflation. They argue, however, that the inflation-targeting framework seems to help maintain an already low rate of inflation in New Zealand and, although communication to the public and transparency and accountability of the process, helps bolster political support for the mandate of price stability.

Bernanke et al. (1999), in the most comprehensive international comparative study to date, reach somewhat stronger conclusions in support of inflation targeting. They argue that a well-structured inflation-targeting regime provides a useful framework for making monetary policy and present proposals to introduce it to the Federal Reserve System and the new European System of Central Banks. They point to transparency and flexibility, properly balanced in operational design, as key elements of successful inflation-targeting regimes.

But is the formalism associated with the new inflation targeting regimes really necessary? Bernanke et al. point out that the traditional German monetary targeting approach employed prior to EMU is not distinguishable in substance from an inflation-targeting regime. Could one conclude from this that "flexible monetarism," in the sense of that practiced by Germany since the early 1970s, amounts to an inflation targeting regime as long as there is an inflation objective and an underlying commitment to price stability on the part of the central bank? Moreover the case of the United States sheds some doubt on whether the particular operating framework of the central bank, whether it be inflation targeting, monetary targeting, or otherwise, is a necessary element in achieving low and stable rates of inflation.

In this context, our reading of the empirical evidence and case studies suggests that inflation targeting is a useful way to communicate to the public the strong and consistent commitment of the central bank to price stability. The transparent method of inflation targeting, especially when complemented by explicit inflation forecasts and timely public reports, sends a strong signal about the seriousness of one's intentions.

In summary, we find four compelling reasons for central banks, including the Bank of Japan, to adopt inflation targets. First, the intentions and objectives of monetary policy are clearer, and the bank's accountability is enhanced. Second, monetary policy could become more flexible and proactive with a inflation target. With a clear, numerical inflation target, the task of explaining monetary policy actions would be easier. Policy changes, if necessary, would not damage the credibility of the central bank as long as they were explained in the context of the stationary inflation target. Third, commitment to a defined inflation target would help the central bank define the parameters of its independence. The central bank would benefit from having the freedom to choose its policy instruments. Other institutions in the government would only be able to hold the central bank responsible if results were not consistent with the announced target. The media could not then blame other institutions for putting "pressure" on the central bank. Last, the very fact of announcing an inflation target likely would have a positive impact on financial markets and the economy as a whole. A 1 to 3 percent target in the Japanese context, for example, would have helped dispel the deflationary uncertainties that prevailed at the end of the 1990s. This would likely have simulated more consumption and investment expenditure and, in turn, making inflationary expectations self-fulfilling even before all the right policy measures had run their course.

When all is said and done, however, actual inflation performance is the ultimate determinant of inflation credibility in any monetary policy regime. The central bank cannot bring credibility to an inflation-targeting regime simply by announcements. Eventually policy measures must be introduced and prove effective in hitting the announced targets. We address this issue in the context of Japanese monetary policy instruments and policy effectiveness in chapter 6.

5.4 The New Bank of Japan and Institutional Features of Inflation Targeting

The 1998 Bank of Japan Law represents the most important change in the institutional structure and legal status of the central bank since its formation in 1882. This has resulted in a substantial increase in the Bank of Japan's institutional independence from other parts of government and also the formal recognition of price stability as a key objective of policy. Three key changes in the Law are relevant in these respects.

First, the 1998 Law narrows the objective of the Bank of Japan to two goals: "the pursuit of price stability, contributing to the sound development of the national economy (Article 2)" and "maintenance of an orderly financial system (Article 1)." Price stability is not specifically defined nor specified as the only policy objective. The absence of references to full employment, economic growth, or exchange rate objectives, however, suggests that price stability at least from an operational perspective is the primary goal of monetary policy along with stability of the financial system. The new Law clearly states that the Bank of Japan is responsible for price stability while the responsibility for financial stability is a shared responsibility with government.

Second, the old Law provided the Bank of Japan with no formal independence and stated explicitly that the Bank of Japan was an instrument of the Ministry of Finance and government in virtually every area of operation. This was most clearly expressed by the authority granted to the Cabinet to dismiss the governor and vice-governor and for the Minister of Finance to dismiss executive directors, auditors, and advisers (Article 47) "whenever it is deemed particularly necessary for the attainment of the objective of the Bank."

The new Law changed this fundamental relationship between the Bank of Japan, Ministry of Finance, and government. The new Law states that "the Bank of Japan's autonomy regarding the currency and monetary control shall be respected (Article 3)," and more generally that "due consideration shall be given to the autonomy of the Bank's business operations." The power to remove Bank of Japan officers has been significantly limited to removal for incompetence, criminal behavior, or incapacity to discharge duties.

Third, the role of the Policy Board was reaffirmed in the 1998 Law. Even under the old Law, the Policy Board theoretically had significant decision-making power. Over time, however, the Policy Board failed to assume this power and instead generally approved whatever the Bank staff through the Executive Board recommended. The Policy Board was reinstated with a different membership composition as the primary policy-making body of the Bank of Japan with respect to currency and monetary control issues.

The newly re-established Policy Board consists of 9 members. There are three representatives of the Bank of Japan: the Bank's governor and two deputy governors. The majority, however, consists of six Deliberative Members selected by the Cabinet with the consent of the Diet among "experts on the economy of finance and academics (Article 23)." The membership of the Policy Board differs significantly from the Policy Board established in 1949. The government has no formal representation on the Policy Board, although, representatives from the Ministry of Finance and the Economic Planning Agency can attend Board meetings to express views and even request a delay in a policy decision (Article 19). Moreover the majority of members (six Deliberative Members) represent a broader viewpoint, since they are to be chosen for their expertise rather than whether they represent a specific sector of the economy. This is quite a contrast to the 1942 Law where the nongovernment representatives were required to represent financial institutions, agriculture, and commerce.

Inflation Targeting at the Bank of Japan in the New Institutional Environment

The new institutional environment at the Bank of Japan would provide an even stronger foundation than previously for the implementation of an inflation-targeting regime and the credible commitment to a positive rate of inflation. Similar to New Zealand and several other countries, Japan's reform gives the central bank a high degree of institutional independence. However, the Bank of Japan has a fair amount of flexibility about setting its own inflation objective. That is, the Bank of Japan has more discretion over policy than, say, New Zealand. But there would be nothing of an institutional nature to hinder the Bank of Japan's Policy Board from introducing an inflation target along the lines of Krugman's 4 percent proposal or some other, presumably lower, target rate.

5.5   Inflation Targeting to Stop Deflation

The focus of almost all the literature on central bank independence and inflation targeting is to establish an institutional framework designed to maintain low and stable rates of inflation against the upward bias created by the myriad of political and economic pressures. During the 1998–2000 period, however, deflation, bank failures and deep recession were the backdrop for the Japanese economy and several other economies in East Asia. Even in Europe, some argued that the "conservative" design of the new European System of Central Banks (i.e., institutionally independent with the primary objective of price stability) may be out of step with the low inflation and high unemployment in the second half of the 1990s.

Swedish Price-Level Targeting in the 1930s

Are the new institutions being established in Europe, Japan, and elsewhere flexible enough to handle deflation as well as inflation? Deflationary experiences are not common, but there is some evidence from the United States in the 1930s. It is clear from the literature that, had the Federal Reserve pursued an inflation target, policy would have been much more stimulative. As it turned out, the tight monetary contraction in the United States at the time exacerbated the initial downturn and banking problems. The reinforcement of monetary contraction, banking collapses and recession led to one of the most serious economic declines in modern history that lasted a decade.[8]

By contrast, Sweden left the gold standard in the fall of 1931 and adopted an explicit price level target (Berg and Jonung 1999). These moves were taken at the onset of the Great Depression with the objective of stopping price deflation. However, price-level targeting also mitigated widespread concerns that abandonment of the gold standard would eventually lead to rising prices. Hence the Swedish case may be the best example to date of how an explicit price- or inflation-targeting regime might work in a deflationary environment such as that faced by Japan in the late 1990s.

Swedish consumer prices had been falling gradually, and wholesale prices sharply, since late 1928 as the workings of the inter-war gold standard transmitted deflationary pressures to Sweden. Industrial production declined by 21 percent during 1929 to 1931 (compared to a fall of 46 percent in the United States during this period), and unem-

---

8. Friedman and Schwartz (1963) played an important role in this development; however, they were not the first to draw attention to the role of monetary policy as a cause of the Great Depression. Friedman and Schwartz made the most detailed argument and the one that generated heated debate that ended with the general consensus that the Federal Reserve (monetary policy in general) was a major cause of the depression and deflation in the 1930s. Cargill and Mayer (1998) provide a review and references to some of this literature.

ployment rose sharply. Against this background, the Swedish Minister of Finance announced in September 1931 that the central bank (Riksbank) was relieved of its legal obligation to convert domestic currency notes into gold upon demand. The new objective for Riksbank policy should be aimed at, using all means available, "preserving the domestic purchasing power of the Swedish krona" (Berg and Jonung 1999, p. 535).

Berg and Jonung present evidence that Swedish policy makers at the time believed that an institutional commitment to price stability could act as a coordinating device and anchor expectations. To this end, key features of the program included a clear and transparent objective, communicated to the public through several channels. The Riksbank published a consumer price index as part of its monetary program but also relied on other price indexes. The central bank's concern was also "underlying inflation," in that it emphasized the need to disregard temporary factors like seasonal effects and customs duties in evaluating the price level. The Swedish Parliament (Riksdag) and its Banking Committee supervised and monitored the Riksbank's activities and issued regular reports. The governor of the Riksbank was questioned annually by the Banking Committee and monitoring of the central bank was an open political process known to the public. In addition to annual examinations by the Banking Committee, two major evaluations of the Riksbank's price-targeting program were conducted in 1933 and 1937.

Similar to the modern New Zealand experience, Sweden's price-targeting program in the 1930s was modified as economic conditions worsened. No legal backing was given to the Swedish program and, although the price-stability objective was maintained, adjustments and additional goals were added by requests from the Parliament and Minister of Finance. In particular, in 1932 the original goals were adjusted as both import prices and domestic market prices were allowed to increase. The Riksbank was also asked to keep interest rates as low as possible and to link monetary policy with fiscal policy measures to combat unemployment.

By most measures, price-level targeting in Sweden in the 1930s was an effective way to stop price deflation and help mitigate the depression. CPI and WPI movements followed similar patterns, but the WPI was much more extreme. The CPI declined between 1928 and 1932–33 and then turned upward. The WPI fell sharply from January 1928 to September 1931 and then remained roughly constant, with minor decline, until spring 1933. The WPI then began a gradual rise until 1937.

The depression in Sweden did not abruptly stop with the introduction of price-level targeting, but the output declines appear to have been mitigated and recovery enhanced by the monetary program. Swedish unemployment rose sharply in 1930 and 1931 and then drifted upward slightly until peaking at over 30 percent in spring 1933. Unemployment then began to fall, reaching a 15 percent level by 1937. Industrial production reached a low point in mid-1932, declining roughly 20 percent from the 1928 level. By the end of 1933, however, Swedish industrial production had recovered to the 1928 level and climbed an additional 28 percent by the end of 1934. Industrial production in the United States, by contrast, fell by almost 50 percent at its trough in 1932 and did not reach the 1928 production level again until the end of 1936.

In terms of the modern literature on inflation targeting, however, Berg and Jonung (1999) point out that there was no discussion of a "forward-looking approach" or an attempt to tie monetary instrument changes to price or inflation forecasts. This is an important element of the modern discussion because of the well-known lags between changes in monetary instruments such as interest rates and monetary growth and changes in the price level.

Japan in the 1930s[9]

Japan's experience during the worldwide depression of the 1930s was generally very favorable once its temporary return to the gold standard was abandoned. The new Japanese government coming into power in July 1929 announced the decision to return to the gold standard, at the prewar par value, at the earliest possible date. Since Japan's wholesale price level was substantially above (by 65 percent) the prewar level than in the United States and England, a deflation was likely to be necessary. Austere fiscal measures and somewhat restrictive monetary policy were adopted and were effective in pushing down wholesale prices—by 6 percent in the second half of 1929 and a continuing decline in 1930. Japan officially returned to the gold standard on January 11, 1930, at the prewar parity of $45 per 100 yen.

---

9. This section draws heavily on Patrick's (1971) excellent discussion of monetary and banking policy in Japan in the 1920s and early 1930s.

Early 1930 may have been the worst possible time to return to the gold standard as the world economy was spiraling into depression and Japan's exports were hard hit (e.g., the market fell sharply for silk in the United States—the single most important export commodity). Japan's economy slumped due to price deflation, austere fiscal policy, and the impact of the world economic collapse. Exports fell, a current account deficit developed, and gold reserves flowed out of Japan. Japan lost more than 59 percent of its gold reserves over the period from when it entered the gold standard and when it left almost two years later in December 1931.

Patrick (1971, p. 256) describes what followed Japan's decision to leave the gold standard as "one of the most successful combinations of fiscal, monetary, and foreign exchange rate policies, in an adverse international environment, that the world has ever seen." Without the external constraint (fixed exchange rate), large-scale deficit financing and an easy monetary policy were implemented. From 1931 to 1933 government spending rose 26 percent and net domestic product jumped at a comparable rate. Expansionary fiscal policy accommodated by monetary policy, together with exchange rate depreciation, generated a boom in domestic demand, encouraged exports, and discouraged imports. The economy once again started to grow quickly.

Most of the rise in government spending was deficit financed and, from 1932 on, the Bank of Japan underwrote the government's bond issues. It purchased outright that portion that had not been subscribed by the Ministry of Finance Deposit Bureau. Patrick (1971) explains how government deficit-financed spending resulted in an increase in commercial bank deposits, and that banks were eager to purchase government bonds from the Bank of Japan since private lending was so limited.

The Bank of Japan did not take positive steps to increase commercial bank reserves but rather stood ready to rediscount upon request. Requests were limited, however, so it did not expand credit greatly to the private sector until the mid-1930s. The money supply increased only moderately until 1937. The Bank of Japan during this period lowered its discount rate far below any previous minimum level—rates stood at 3.29 percent in 1936 compared with 6.57 percent at the end of 1931. Other interest rates followed suite. Lowered interest rates and easy money supported the resurgent economy.

Japan's decisions to leave the gold standard and pursue expansionary fiscal and monetary policy allowed the economy to expand vigorously through most of the 1930s. Unlike Sweden, there was no commitment to price level targeting. But allowing the exchange rate to depreciate effectively stopped domestic deflation. After falling about 30 percent in 1930–31, wholesales prices rose 28 percent in Japan over the next two years (1932–33). By contrast, wholesale prices continued to fall in the United States (11 percent) and the United Kingdom (2 percent) during 1932 and 1933. Japan's exchange rate declined almost 40 percent, from 0.488 yen per U.S.$ to 0.295 yen per U.S.$ between 1931 and 1934.

5.6   Would Inflation Targeting Have Stopped Japan's Deflation?

The Bank of Japan was given substantially greater independence in 1998 not with the intent of lowering inflation, but following complex political maneuvering whereby the Ministry of Finance attempted to shield itself from further reforms on the regulatory and supervisory side of its operations. As it turned out, central bank and financial supervision and regulatory reform was wide sweeping amid the scandals at the Ministry of Finance and its mishandling of the banking crisis.

Similarly the proposal to institute a form of inflation targeting at the Bank of Japan would also be in sharp contrast to recent reforms in other countries that have been directed toward inflation control. Rather, the concern in the late 1990s in Japan—and the objective of the inflationary targeting proposal—would be to counter price deflation, stagnation and a potential liquidity trap situation. As with Sweden in the early 1930s, the objective would be to provide a credible and transparent nominal anchor so that the private sector expected either price stability or low inflation, but definitely not deflation.

There is a strong theoretical argument for some form of inflation targeting, but in practice, it appears that a strong commitment to low inflation such as that epitomized by the German Bundesbank may work as well as the more formal legal and institutional approach followed, for example, by New Zealand. Germany, however, has strong public and political support for low inflation rooted in its prewar history. An inflation-targeting regime may help central banks help countries lower the rate of inflation while maintaining price stability in the face of adverse shocks and political pressures.

We have much less experience with inflation targeting regimes in times of price deflation. The Swedish case is instructive, however, and suggests that inflation targeting may be an important institutional mechanism to help stabilize expectations in a period of recession and falling prices. Although the Japanese economy in the late 1990s was not in a severe depression and facing a worldwide collapse in production and trade, some insights from the Swedish case in the 1930s may be drawn as well as Japan's own history in the 1930s. In particular, the counterfactual policy stance, if the Bank of Japan had been following inflation targeting, it would presumably have made an even more aggressive attempt at monetary stimulus than that actually followed.

The Bank of Japan responded to the continued slump by increasing liquidity, partly by repo arrangements with commercial banks. The objective presumably was an attempt to ease the credit crunch by indirect injections of liquidity into the corporate sector. However, liquidity creation was also expected find its way into the banking system, eventually increasing bank reserves and base money.

There appears no compelling case against the Bank of Japan pursuing a more aggressive approach in extending credit in the late 1990s. This would have been an appropriate policy response for either a liquidity trap or a credit crunch situation. Other instruments remain to inject liquidity into the economy. The Bank of Japan could, for example, have purchased long-term government bonds. Japan's Fiscal Law prohibits the Bank of Japan from purchasing new bond issues directly from the Ministry of Finance; however, the law does allow the Bank of Japan to purchase long bonds issued one year or more in the past in the secondary market.

One objection to this practice might be that the central banks in principle should not risk capital losses associated with long-term debt instruments. This seems a small risk, however, given that the Bank could hold the bonds to maturity and that its operating profits are in any case transferred to the government. Many central banks take positions in longer-term government debt instruments. The Federal Reserve System in the United States, for example, undertook significant purchases of long-term government bonds in the early 1960s in an attempt to influence the yield curve then referred to as "operation twist" policy.

This course of action is entirely consistent with an inflation targeting approach. Inflation targeting may be symmetric and equally applicable to situations of deflation as well as inflation. Sweden introduced a price-level targeting regime to counter the deflation of the 1930s (and later the concern that long-term inflation may be a threat without an operative gold standard as the nominal anchor). If the Bank of Japan had been following an inflation targeting regime in 1997 to 1999, say targeting the CPI in a range between 1 to 3 percent, it would had attempted an even more expansionary stance than that actually followed. Near deflation in the CPI would have triggered a stronger policy response than the relatively passive stance pursued by the Bank of Japan.

On the surface, our argument appears consistent with Krugman's proposal that the Bank of Japan should have deliberately raised inflation expectations. However, our argument is that stability of inflation expectations is an important long-run objective, not a temporary quick fix to recession and deflation. Nonetheless, it seems clear that introducing an inflation targeting regime in the late 1990s would have induced the Bank of Japan to follow a more expansionary policy stance. A more expansionary monetary policy would have broken the vicious cycle of expected deflation, recession, high real interest rates, and increasing debt-burden on borrowers.

5.7   Concluding Comments

Japan's economic conditions in the late 1990s were qualitatively similar to those experienced by a number of countries in the 1930s. While Japan did not experience the economic and financial collapse experienced in the 1930s, the similarities are striking. Deflation, stagnant and declining growth, low interest rates with short-term rates close to zero, and an inability of monetary policy to stimulate aggregate demand. The liquidity trap saw renewed discussion after laying dorminent for several decades. The liquidity trap had been frequently invoked in the 1950s and 1960s as an explanation of why monetary policy in the United States and United Kingdom was ineffective in stimulating aggregate demand in the 1930s.

The liquidity trap debate combined with the adoption of formal inflation targeting frameworks by a number of developed and developing countries suggested that Japan's situation could benefit from a consideration of inflation targeting. Inflation targeting was being adopted by a number of countries as a means to control inflation, but the Japanese experience and the liquidity trap debate suggested the benefits of inflation targeting were symmetrical. That is, inflation targeting would be a useful framework to prevent both inflation and deflation.

The economic and financial conditions of the Japanese economy appear consistent with a liquidity trap concept; however, other explanations focused on banking problems and changes in regulatory environment cannot be dismissed. Inappropriate fiscal policy in 1997 also played a contributing role. We suggest that other explanations are more likely, including the fact that monetary policy in Japan was not as simulative as conditions warranted.

Independent of the liquidity trap debate, many economists argued in the late 1990s that the Bank of Japan would benefit from an explicit inflation target to reverse deflation. There were no significant obstacles to such a policy. The Swedish experience in the 1930s and Japan's own experience in the 1930s suggest that inflation targeting would have been a useful policy in the late 1990s.

Inflation targeting has received much attention in the past decade and a number of developed and developing countries have adopted some form of explicit targeting. The context, however, has been to prevent inflation. Japan provides a case study that suggests inflation targeting is also useful to prevent deflation.

6   Challenges Facing Financial Policy and Central Banking in Japan

6.1   Introduction

This concluding chapter discusses the challenges to financial policy and central banking faced by Japan as the country enters the new century. During the 1990s, Japan experienced its worst financial crisis and deepest recession of the postwar period. These effects are still being felt, but at the same time the authorities are faced with new challenges following the shift to a new financial supervision and regulation structure, changes in the structure of the financial system, and changes in the Bank of Japan Law. We first discuss some key challenges in the design and implementation of financial policy, some of which are related to the new financial supervision and regulation framework. We then turn to challenges facing the Bank of Japan as it adapts to the new institutional framework established by the change in the central bank law.

These issues are closely related. Unless Japan can adapt its financial supervision and regulation framework to foster a more stable financial system, problems in this area will continue to limit the ability of the Bank of Japan to pursue a policy consistent with steady and sustained economic growth. There is little doubt financial distress in the 1990s had significant real effects on the economy that were exacerbated by an apparent liquidity trap faced by monetary policy in 1998 and 1999. By the same token, failure of the new Bank of Japan to achieve price stability, especially preventing the type of deflation experienced in the late 1990s, make it difficult for the new financial supervision and regulation regime to deal with financial distress. Further, once the deflation and financial distress problems are solved, it will become easier to implement and find political support for continued financial liberalization so as to achieve the objectives stated in the 1996 Big Bang announcement.

6.2   The New Financial Supervision and Regulation Framework

The new financial supervision and regulation framework evolving in Japan will face five major challenges in the near future: dealing with a large number of weak financial institutions (and associated non-performing loans), implementing a more explicit deposit guarantee system, resolution of the extensive system of government financial intermediation associated with the Fiscal Loan and Investment Program (FILP), adapting to structural changes that are very likely to shrink the size of the banking sector further in the years to come, and maintaining the independence of the Financial Supervisory Agency from both the Ministry of Finance and the government in general. Each of these will be elaborated in turn.

Dealing with Financial Distress

A key challenge facing the new financial supervisory and regulatory institutions at the beginning of the new century is to resolve the large nonperforming loan problem. This issue continued to cast a shadow over Japan's financial system and exacerbated the credit crunch in the latter part of the 1990s. By October 1998 Japan had committed 60 trillion yen of public funds to resolve the problem, an amount large enough to make sufficient headway in recapitalizing banks and writing off non-performing loans. Combined with the institutional changes made to the Deposit Insurance Corporation and the establishment of new institutions formally independent of the Ministry of Finance, the infusion of public monies has the potential to sharply reduce financial distress. In addition Japan formally adopted a "trip wire" type regulatory structure (Prompt Corrective Action) designed to reduce some of the regulatory discretion by requiring certain actions based on the capital asset ratio of the bank. Viewed in broad perspective and compared to the type of financial regime in place throughout much of postwar Japan, these changes are impressive and combined with the commitment of public funding should be sufficient to deal with the current financial distress.

An important issue is whether the new framework will be accompanied by a fundamental change in the approach taken to resolve

financial distress and help to prevent similar problems from arising in the future. A new approach is needed to deal with problems as
they arise in an expeditious way and with greater accountability and
transparency. An orderly process also needs to be implemented to
more aggressively dispose of nonperforming loans, and most importantly, to more quickly recapitalize, restructure and close problem
financial institutions. Japan has a window of opportunity that will
soon close when features of the 1998 bailout legislation will expire after
March 2001, the complete government deposit guarantee is removed,
and the payoff cost limit is reimposed on the Deposit Insurance
Corporation.

Government Deposit Guarantees: Implicit versus Explicit

At the beginning stage of the financial crisis in 1995, the Japanese government announced that it would guarantee all bank deposits despite
the deposit insurance law's stipulation that the fund would only cover
up to 10 million yen per customer per bank. This covered not only bank
deposits, but also bank debentures issued by long-term credit banks
(since small investors directly hold bank debentures).

The announcement was meant to calm down worries among depositors that some banks would be closed and liquidated. The blanket
guarantee had the intended effect, and at the height of banking crisis in
1997 there was no panicky response by depositors. However, deposits
tended to move out of weaker institutions at certain critical points.
Hokkaido Takushoku Bank, for example, is said to have lost deposits
of 200 billion yen in the month of September 1997, two months before
its collapse. In addition deposits continued to shift from the banking
system to the postal savings system (Cargill and Yoshino 2000).

There are two main problems in implementing deposit insurance.
First, it is difficult to consolidate one customer's various accounts in different branches of a single (failed) financial institution. The law
stipulates that the ceiling is per customer per bank. Namely all the
accounts, possibly in many branches, should in principle be consolidated. Since there is no system requiring a taxpayer number (social security number), it is difficult, both in time and manpower required, to consolidate these accounts. Second, liquidating an insolvent institution,
and paying depositors up to 10 million yen each on their consolidated
accounts, may still require financial support from the government to
cover these and other liabilities. However, it was politically difficult to

obtain support from the Diet for a commitment to bailing out financial institutions before November 1997. How the funds committed in 1998 would be used would determine whether the public would continue to support further capital injections from the government to resolve the banking distress. The results of the first injection of public funds to the banking system in March 1998 were disappointing while the second injection in March 1999 showed a more aggressive approach.

The difficulty in implementing the deposit insurance "payoff option" made the regulatory authorities hesitant to close institutions, even for the clearly insolvent cases in 1994 and 1995. Instead, the authorities sought to arrange mergers whereby a healthy institution would take over weak institutions as part of a general approach to financial distress based on mutual support. Alternatively, they sought collective subscriptions of new equities either to set up an institution to assume assets and liabilities of failed institutions (in the case of Tokyo Kyodo Bank), or to directly assist a weak institution (in the case of Nippon Credit Bank).

The deposit insurance system therefore did not work to cap depositors' claims in failed institutions, since only liquidation, or payoffs, could trigger the deposit insurance limit. In the case of a merger or a collective rescue, all deposits were protected. But the Deposit Insurance Corporation's outlay to a white knight institution was limited to the payoff equivalent.

Although the government protected all deposits, regardless of the insurance system's ceiling, this policy is slated to change after March 31, 2002. A new system is scheduled to be introduced to make the deposit insurance system workable. Weaker institutions could face a loss of deposits as this date nears, however. Therefore, strengthening the capital base and restructuring must be completed before the deposit insurance ceiling is re-imposed (referred to as "reintroduction of payoff"). This is one of the reasons that the reintroduction of payoff was delayed by one year to April 2002. Certain safeguards are being considered together with the planned implementation of the deposit insurance ceilings. Recommended safeguards include a smooth transition of deposits from a failed institution to the acquiring institution, and continuous service of payment settlements. This implies that Prompt Corrective Action through 2001 would need to clean up weaker institutions, thereby reducing the size of the problem by the time of the policy change. In any case, some kind of revision in deposit insurance system is needed before March 2002.

The Role of Government Financial Intermediation

Government regulation and administration of the flow of funds to support industrial policy has historically been an important element in Japan's financial system. Japan in the postwar period developed a multidimensional and complex institutional arrangement of postal savings offices and government financial institutions designed to transfer funds from the public to designated sectors of the economy. The system is referred to as the Fiscal Investment and Loan Program (FILP) system. It is under the control of the Ministry of Finance, receiving and distributing funds through its Trust Fund Bureau. The postal savings system provides about 25 percent of the total sources of FILP funding. The FILP then transfers the funds to 10 government banks that make subsidized loans to targeted sectors of the economy as well as a variety of government corporations and enterprises. In terms of deposit size, the postal savings system is the world's largest financial institution with 241 trillion yen in deposits. In 1998, postal deposits accounted for 36 percent of total bank deposits and the market share of the postal savings system has continually increased since 1991 (table 6.1). The postal savings system also sells life insurance, which like postal deposits, represents a major market share (31 percent in 1998, table 6.1).

The postal savings system and the FILP have resisted reform during the past two decades of financial liberalization while other parts of the Japanese financial system have become more competitive and market oriented. As such, the FILP system has become a serious constraint on financial liberalization in general and unless meaningful reform takes place, will limit the success of the new financial supervision and regulatory framework evolving in Japan. The postal saving system in particular has played a destabilizing role in the 1990s (Cargill 1993b; Cargill and Yoshino 2000). It has complicated Japan's deposit guarantee system and been responsible for periods of disintermediation from bank to postal deposits as the public became aware of nonperforming loan problems in private banks. Disintermediation resulted from the public's trust in the government guarantee of postal saving and distrust on banks' health, despite the same degree of announced deposit guarantee on deposits in the postal saving system and banks. In 1994 an agreement was reached between the regulatory authorities and the postal savings system to the effect that the postal saving system would henceforth set deposit rates "close to" private bank deposit rates to reduce the competitive pressure on private financial institutions. How-

Table 6.1
Postal savings and life insurance and private bank deposits and life insurance (100 million yen)

Fiscal year	Total deposits	Postal deposits	Postal as percentage of total	Total life insurance	Postal life insurance	Postal as percentage of total
1980	1,855,070	519,116	28.0	470,450	114,534	24.4
1981	2,078,724	619,543	29.8	527,186	133,508	25.3
1982	2,314,110	695,676	30.1	608,530	154,308	25.4
1983	2,525,205	781,026	30.9	699,768	178,319	25.5
1984	2,722,205	862,982	31.7	801,627	203,977	25.5
1985	2,942,360	940,421	32.0	912,174	231,820	25.4
1986	3,180,054	1,029,979	32.4	804,551	239,872	29.8
1987	3,401,636	1,103,952	32.5	943,809	290,087	30.7
1988	3,658,950	1,173,908	32.1	1,101,850	325,876	29.6
1989	3,937,885	1,258,691	32.0	1,291,025	368,471	28.5
1990	4,360,835	1,345,723	30.9	1,513,600	415,102	27.4
1991	4,688,454	1,362,804	29.1	1,726,042	464,156	26.9
1992	5,034,967	1,550,470	30.8	1,905,014	517,835	27.2
1993	5,280,704	1,700,906	32.2	2,096,031	578,173	27.6
1994	5,549,690	1,835,348	33.1	2,328,005	655,311	28.2
1995	5,872,459	1,975,902	33.7	2,587,471	743,450	28.7
1996	6,133,435	2,134,375	34.8	2,831,675	842,030	29.7
1997	6,397,098	2,248,872	35.2	3,119,091	941,864	30.2
1998	6,741,353	2,405,460	35.7	3,296,552	1,007,720	30.6

Sources: Ministry of Posts and Telecommunications, *Annual Statistics*, and Bank of Japan, *Economic Statistics Annual*.

ever, the interest rate offered on postal saving deposits is still higher than offered by private banks.

The Big Bang announcement in November 1996, despite its broad agenda, did not mention the postal savings system or make any meaningful reference to FILP reform. Their omission from the announcement suggested official reluctance to deal with one of the most important constraints on financial modernization. In fact during this period the postal savings system in Japan was being held up as a model for other Asian countries (*Wall Street Journal*, April 18, 1997). In the spring of 1997, a flurry of legislation was passed to begin implementation of the Big Bang objectives; however, there were no proposals to deal with the postal savings system or the FILP. It was clear, however, that the postal saving system would soon be on the agenda for structural reform—especially since its relative importance in the financial system had increased during the past two decades despite an official policy of liberalization. Moreover, until the 1994 deposit rate setting agreement, the postal saving system had not been subjected to any significant reform.[1]

The FILP system has recently become the object of reform, however. As part of the Laws to Reform Central Government Ministries and Agencies passed June 1998, the structure of government budgeting was fundamentally changed (Cargill and Yoshino 1998). Starting in March 2001, the government will no longer receive funds from the postal savings system. Postal savings funds will be managed independently. Government financial institutions will issue their own bonds, but with a government guarantee just like regular government bonds.

Postal deposits have increased their market share in recent years (table 6.1) and loans from some government banks in the late 1990s expanded in response to the credit crunch at the private banks. Figure 6.1 illustrates loan growth at the People's Finance Corporation and the Japan Finance Corporation for Small Business. Loans from these two government banks increased in 1998 in contrast to the credit crunch at private banks (figure 2.5). An irony is that credit crunch among private-sector banks necessitated actions by the government, which contradicted the goal of reducing the extent of government financial intermediation. Despite an official policy of liberalization, the growth of public intermediation presents serious challenges for the new regulatory and supervisory regime emerging in Japan.

Structural Changes as Financial Liberalization Continues

Japan's traditional financial regime was based on "bank finance" with little meaningful role allocated to the capital market or direct finance generally. The bank-dominated model not only characterized the flow of funds but influenced the institutional and policy orientation of the supervision and regulation framework. The framework was designed to protect and ensure both the viability and growth of the banking sys-

---

1. The Tax Reform Act of 1986 did indirectly influence the postal savings system by eliminating the interest income tax deduction up to 3 million yen. The post office had blatantly allowed depositors to violate the rule and maintain multiple deposits totaling far more than 3 million yen.

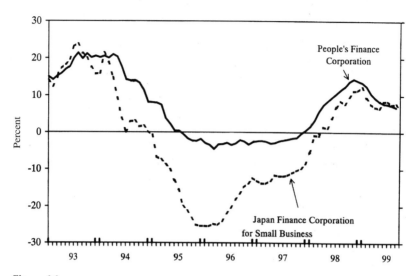

Figure 6.1
Lending for small businesses: People's Finance Corporation and Japan Finance Corporation for Small Business. Source: Bank of Japan, *Monthly Report of Recent Economic and Financial Developments*, November 1999.

tem. The growth of money and capital markets and the decline of the market share held by banks has been a distinctive feature of financial liberalization in Japan. This process places banks under great competitive pressure, and it creates serious challenges to regulatory authorities and politicians to manage a smooth financial transition. Banks have lost significant market share, and according to recent estimates developed by Hoshi and Kashyap (1999), bank loan demand could conservatively decline by more than 20 percent using the United States as a benchmark and focusing only on demand for funds by large businesses. Hoshi and Kashyap argue that Japan will experience a significant contraction in the banking industry over the next decade under almost any reasonable modeling scenario. As such, the sharp contraction in bank market share will present a financial supervision and regulation framework wedded to the bank finance model with difficult economic and political challenges.

Independence of the Financial Supervision and Regulation Framework

The Financial Supervisory Agency commenced operations June 22, 1998. At first, many observers anticipated that the new institution would remain dependent on the Ministry of Finance as the Ministry provided the majority of staff, guidance, and had had the opportunity to influence the enabling legislation. In addition the Financial Supervisory Agency is required to interact with the Ministry in dealing with troubled institutions as well as other ministries in regard to nonbank depository institutions under their jurisdiction.

The initial concerns appear to have been too pessimistic. The Financial Supervisory Agency has shown a high degree of independence and willingness to break away from the past Ministry of Finance policies of slow response in dealing with insolvent or nonviable financial institutions and non transparency in the reporting of nonperforming loans. One factor supporting this independence is that high-ranking Financial Supervisory Agency officials cannot return to employment at the Ministry of Finance. This independent stance and willingness to develop its own record will likely become stronger over time. The creation of the Financial Reconstruction Commission as part of the Prime Minister's Office further suggests independence from the Ministry of Finance for the Financial Supervisory Agency.

There remains a problem, however. While securing a degree of independence from the Ministry of Finance, there is a concern that the new financial supervision and regulatory framework may become sensitive to direct political influence. It has been decided and implemented that a Minister (that is, a politician) is at the top of Financial Supervisory Agency. Therefore it is conceivable that if the Minister in charge of the Financial Supervisory Agency decided to follow a political agenda instead of asserting Financial Supervisory Agency principles to the rest of the cabinet, the independence of the Agency may be compromised.

Milhaupt (1999) provides insight into the potential political problems facing the new regulatory framework in his discussion of the political debate over the October 1998 legislation establishing the new resolution procedures. Milhaupt concludes that key aspects of the legislation that incorporated more transparency and a greater concern with market discipline were due to the opposition party rather than the LDP. The LDP was forced to go along with the more aggressive legislation when it lost its majority in the Upper House July 1998 and Prime Minister Hashimoto resigned.

The Financial Reconstruction Commission was established October 1998 as part of the Prime Minister's Office to administer the new system for resolving insolvent banks through December 2000 and oversee the Financial Supervisory Agency. The Commission is responsible for identifying insolvent banks based on supervision reports prepared by the Financial Supervisory Agency and the Agency suggests which one of the two ways the insolvency is to be resolved. The insolvent bank can either be operated by a public administrator as a "bridge bank" to continue with normal operations until a suitable merger partner is located or the insolvent bank can be nationalized and placed under public management. It is unknown at this time to what extent, if any, political considerations will become a central element of the work of the Financial Reconstruction Commission. However, a swift process to nationalize the Nippon Credit Bank dispelled any doubt that the Financial Supervisory Agency would be influenced by the Ministry of Finance or by politicians.

The subject of independence for the new financial supervision and regulation framework provides a convenient stopping point at which we can turn our attention to challenges facing the new Bank of Japan.

6.3   Scandal and Uncertainty at the Bank of Japan

April 1, 1998, was to have been an historic and festive moment for the Bank of Japan. The Bank of Japan had finally secured independence from the Ministry of Finance, a goal sought after for decades. The major change in the new Bank of Japan Law was reform of the Policy Board that would formulate monetary policy independently of the Ministry of Finance and government. The new Policy Board consists of nine members with the Bank of Japan represented by the governor and two deputy governors.

The atmosphere at the start of new Bank of Japan and Policy Board, however, was somber. Despite the achievement of political and institutional independence, the Bank of Japan and the Policy Board started in the most difficult period of the entire postwar period for monetary policy. Three reasons can be identified for this somber mood.

First, financial scandals revealed in 1997 engulfed the Bank of Japan, as well as the Ministry of Finance, resulting in the surprise resignations of the governor and deputy governor a month before the new Bank of Japan became effective April 1, 1998. Several Bank of Japan officers were rumored to have been lavishly entertained by private sector bankers. After an investigation, one Bank of Japan official was arrested for leaking confidential information to private-sector participants prior to Bank of Japan actions and news releases, and many officials were reprimanded through internal channels. Governor Matsushita and Senior Deputy Governor Fukui resigned, accepting responsibility for the scandal. Since Deputy Governor Fukui was heir apparent for the governor position, his resignation was also of central importance and indicated the levels to which the scandal within the Bank of Japan had reached.

Second, the economy was experiencing deflation and a deepening recession after almost a decade of economic stagnation. Real GDP declined in the fourth quarter of 1997. Asset prices were declining and aggregate demand was weak, even after a series of fiscal stimulus packages and an apparently easy monetary policy stance. The official discount rate had been lowered to a historic level of 0.5 percent and narrow money (M1) increased by almost 14 percent in 1996 and 9 percent in 1997. There was a sense that monetary policy was ineffective at this point and had done all that was possible to stimulate the economy.

The new Bank of Japan and the new Policy Board had to work in an environment for which they had no recent precedent. Price deflation is very rare in modern industrial economies. The role of monetary policy in this environment was difficult at best, and the Bank of Japan had no clear direction to follow. Some argued that monetary policy had become ineffective and caught in a liquidity trap, while others suggested that the central bank had not done enough to expand the money supply. The Bank of Japan had earned an international reputation as a price stabilizing central bank in the 1980s. Because of its seeming inability to reverse the economic decline and deflation, however, the Bank of Japan faced questions about its policy course.

Third, Japan was in the midst of a serious financial crisis. The nonperforming loan problem had not been resolved despite a series of policy actions including deposit insurance reform, liquidation of the housing finance (*jusen*) industry, and bank recapitalization in March 1998 with fiscal funds. On the eve of the start of the new Bank of Japan the financial distress sharply increased with the failure of Hokkaido Takushoku Bank and Yamaichi Securities Company. The Bank of Japan was forced to seriously consider risk to the entire banking system, or what is referred to as "systemic risk," as it formulated and executed monetary and financial policy.

6.4   Bank of Japan Morale, Human Capital, and Political Pressure

Recent developments have posed challenges to the Bank of Japan in terms of supporting the morale and training and retention of staff, as well as its ability to maintain its independence from political pressure.

Morale at the Bank of Japan

Morale among Bank of Japan staff suffered in 1998 and 1999 in the face of scandal and, with the new Bank of Japan Law, less opportunity to reach the top echelons of policy making and in some cases reduced compensation and benefits. Promotion to an executive director position had been viewed as a high point of a Bank of Japan career. The Policy Board replaced the Executive Board of Directors as the top policy-making body, however, leaving Bank of Japan staff with less opportunity to play a key role in formulating policy.

Outside scrutiny of the Bank of Japan's management was part of the process leading to revision of the 1942 Bank of Japan Law. Accountability and transparency were emphasized in return for independence. Bank staff compensation and benefits were openly criticized in the news media. Salary levels of Bank of Japan staff were roughly in line with those paid by large private-sector banks, and were criticized as excessive for quasi-government employees. As part of the independence discussion, Bank of Japan officials agreed that future compensation increases would be moderated and, in some cases, current levels lowered. The scrutiny and criticism was also directed to benefits such as large houses made available to branch managers. Public revelation of the compensation and benefits earned by Bank of Japan management had an adverse effect on the Bank's public reputation. Lower compensation and reduced benefits appears to have been the price paid for greater Bank of Japan independence.

Human Capital

Personnel policies are an important challenge facing the new Bank of Japan. Success in maintaining and enhancing its human capital will place the Bank of Japan in a better position to operate in the new environment. Success in this endeavor will improve internal morale, provide the Bank of Japan with the type of human capital that will be increasingly needed as financial distress gives way to liberalization and stability, and better enable the Bank of Japan to deal with the new Policy Board and the Diet. The maintenance and enhancement of human capital in the Bank of Japan will be an important foundation in building competency in the Bank of Japan to conduct the type of independent monetary policy that has finally been legally granted.

This challenge can be met in several ways. The Bank of Japan may need to reform the policy, widespread among Japanese ministries and large corporations, of internal promotion based on length of service. More emphasis may also be needed on the development of specialized human capital in the areas of advanced risk management of financial products, recruitment, and the utilization of outside experts for high staff positions. Greater flexibility should also be considered in allowing staff members to move to academic, private, or research positions if it contributes to their technical expertise and professional development.

Political Pressure and Central Bank Independence

A strong professional staff is central in establishing a new working relationship with the Diet, where now the Bank of Japan is operating without the institutional insulation previously provided by the Ministry of Finance. The independence of the Bank of Japan requires it to deal directly with the Diet and its legislators. Previously, the Bank of Japan had dealt with the Ministry of Finance and not with politicians directly.

The new environment has created two challenges for the Bank of Japan. First, politicians are likely to have a different set of priorities, less understanding of the details of economic and monetary issues, and less permanence (higher turnover rate) than officials at the Ministry of Finance. This creates a new situation for which the Bank of Japan has little experience. Second, the Bank of Japan is required to establish new political relationships in an environment where its standing and reputation have been diminished by scandal and the perceived ineffectiveness of monetary policy.

These two issues will be sorted out over a period of time as Bank of Japan staff and the Diet interact on policy formulation. Of much longer term consideration, however, is how the overall conduct of the monetary policy—and the insulation of the Bank of Japan from short-term political pressures—will be affected by the legal change in its relationship with the Ministry of Finance and the closer relationship with the Diet.

Cargill, Hutchison, and Ito, (1997) demonstrate that the Bank of Japan achieved an element of de facto political and institutional independence in the mid-1970s and that this contributed to the good inflation performance in Japan. The impressive inflation performance is a matter of record. However, there are several alternative complementary explanations as to how a formally dependent central bank—as written in the Bank of Japan Law of 1942—could have achieved this degree of price stability. One explanation is that the Bank of Japan became quite skillful in its direct persuasion of the Ministry of Finance and, through this channel, was able to convince the government and Diet that the pursuit of price stability should be a policy priority. The Bank of Japan relied on the high inflation problem of 1973 and 1974 as a reminder that political interference would result in adverse consequences.

A second explanation is that the Ministry of Finance became a benevolent protector of the Bank of Japan from political meddling. Although vested interest groups may desire political intervention on policy, the Ministry of Finance, as a group of technocrats, fended off the pressure from legislators. So long as fiscal objectives and monetary objectives did not conflict, the Ministry of Finance was willing to insulate the Bank of Japan from political pressures arising from the Diet to pursue more inflationary policies.

A third explanation considered in detail by Cargill, Hutchison, and Ito (1997) draws on the special features of the Japanese political system and bureaucracy through most of the postwar period. They argue that the dominance of the single-party system (by the LDP) and concentration of power in the hands of a stable, entrenched and insular bureaucracy (e.g., the Ministry of Finance) led to a credible commitment to a long-run policy focus ("reputational equilibrium").

These explanations have implications beyond academic curiosity. According to the first explanation, achieving legal independence simply meant that the legal framework caught up with what had been achieved in practice. If correct, the new Bank of Japan's monetary policy should not be drastically different than that conducted before legal independence was achieved.

By contrast, the second and third explanations imply that gaining central bank independence and the breakdown on the traditional single-party system in Japan may create a more inflationary monetary policy. Less commitment to price stability than in the past could result from the fact that the Bank of Japan now must directly deal with the Diet. The governor, according to the 1998 Bank of Japan Law, is required to report to the Diet at least twice a year, much in the same way the Federal Reserve is required to report to Congress twice a year as required by the Humphrey-Hawkins Act of 1978. In practice, the Bank of Japan has been required to report to the Diet more often than the minimum twice a year requirement. The lack of experience of the Bank of Japan may make it susceptible to pressure from the Diet, and its independence will no doubt be sorely tested over the next few years.

6.5   Short-Run Monetary Policy Challenges: Recession and Deflation

The Japanese economy appeared to stop deteriorating at the end of 1999, but the past decade, as a whole, was the most difficult period for Japanese policy since the beginning of postwar reconstruction. The economy stagnated for much of the decade. The first half of the decade was characterized by asset price deflation, which caused large nonperforming loans in the construction and real estate industries. By the mid-1990s, nonperforming loans weakened balance sheets of all banks. A near crisis developed in the fall of 1997, and negative GDP growth followed due to loss of confidence among consumers and corporations. The credit crunch and declining output caused bankruptcies. However, these problems were not addressed decisively until 1999. The second half of the 1990s can thus be characterized as "deflation," quite a new phenomenon for an industrial country.

The low positive CPI-inflation rate was in reality "deflation" because of the well-known upward biases in the CPI index. Studies by the Bank of Japan suggest an upward bias of roughly 1 percent per annum in the Japan-CPI index (Shiratsuka 1999), suggesting that consumer prices de facto fell by about 1 percent a year in the second half of the 1990s. By the end of the 1990s, the Bank of Japan targeted the call rate at almost zero, and short-term and long-term interest rates were at historic lows. Yields on long-term bonds were about 1.5 percent. Despite low interest rates in the second half of the 1990s, money growth (M2 + CDs) averaged only about 3 percent compared to 7 to 10 percent in the 1980s.

The Japanese authorities in the late 1990s faced one of their most serious economic challenges in the postwar period. What went wrong? What could the Bank of Japan have done to expand the economy more quickly?

The immediate cause of the sharp downturn in 1997 is clear. An increase in the consumption tax rate from 3 percent to 5 percent combined with an end to a temporary income tax cut in April 1997 amounted to a tax increase by 9 trillion yen representing about 1.7 percent of 1997 GDP. This pulled the economy down from the moderate recovery experienced in 1996. The fiscal contraction was compounded by a credit crunch caused by massive nonperforming loans accumulating in the financial system. Banks were attempting to increase their risk-adjusted capital ratios while writing down nonperforming loans.

Less than candid reporting by both banks and the Ministry of Finance about the magnitude of the nonperforming loan problem made it difficult for banks to raise capital in domestic and international financial markets. Banks were thus forced to respond by a sharp contraction in bank lending and thus, imposed a "credit crunch" on the economy.

By any standard, the economic and financial condition of the Japanese economy at the end of the 1990s was perilous, posing the most difficult environment imaginable for the Bank of Japan to begin operations under its new charter. Specific issues facing the Bank of Japan included the possible existence of a liquidity trap and credit crunch, sharp exchange rate fluctuations, whether to more aggressively monetize government bonds, and whether to pursue credit allocation policies. The liquidity trap, credit crunch, nonperforming loan problem explanations, for the Japanese recession and deflation were discussed in detail in chapter 5. The question we address in the next sections is how the Bank of Japan responded to the 1997 to 1999 recession and deflation, how the Bank of Japan could have pursued a more expansionary policy, whether monetary expansion would have been effective in pulling Japan out of recession sooner, and the merits of the Bank of Japan adopting an inflation target.

Recession and Continued Deflation, 1997 to 1999

Real GDP declined rapidly from the last quarter of 1997 and through 1998, recovered somewhat in the first half of 1999 and deteriorated later in the year. The yen depreciated after Japanese financial markets went into turmoil in November 1997 (figure 6.2) from 125 in November 1997 to 145 in August 1998. The CPI declined from November 1997 to the summer of 1998. The CPI inflation rate from April 1997 to March 1998 in fact masked deflation because of the one-time hike in the consumption tax increase in April 1997. In short, from November 1997 to the summer of 1998, Japanese banks experienced difficulties raising foreign funds (mainly U.S. dollars) and Japan's economy was in the process of a deflationary spiral, What could the Bank of Japan have done differently? Could an inflation target have helped guide the Bank of Japan better than the policies the Bank followed?

On April 1, 1998, when the new Bank of Japan began operations with a considerable strengthening of its statutory independence, the call (interbank) rate was around 0.40 to 0.45 percent. The official discount rate remained at 0.50 percent since September 1995. The call rate was maintained in the 0.40 to 0.50 percent range through the summer.

Figure 6.2
Yen-dollar exchange rate: 1990 to 1999. Monthly average of daily interbank central rate in the Tokyo market. Source: Toyo Keizai Shinpo, Inc.

On September 9, 1998, the Bank of Japan lowered the target value of the call rate to around 0.25 percent. This action represented the first significant change in monetary policy in three years. The last significant change occurred September 8, 1995, when the official discount rate was lowered from 1.0 to 0.5 percent. The decision to lower the call rate was based on the recognition that the economy was declining rather than remaining stagnant and the real risk of a deflationary spiral. Intense international pressure was also being exerted on Japan to adopt easier monetary and fiscal policy.

The lowering of the call rate was not sufficient to stimulate the economy. In October 1998 the yen suddenly appreciated from the mid-130s to mid-110s, due to unwinding of hedge funds' yen carry trade. The unwinding was prompted by the changes in risk assessment among the emerging markets. The Russian default in August 1998 and the de facto failure of Long-Term Capital Management in September 1998 drastically changed the capital flows around the yen. Many hedge funds had shorted the yen to invest in emerging market securities and currencies. Those hedge funds that shorted the yen bought back the yen to square their positions and hence, the yen appreciated.

The appreciation of the yen would have made it easier for the Bank of Japan to adopt a more aggressive policy since the Bank would not need to be concerned with an overdepreciation of the yen. The economy was also deteriorating rapidly, further calling for more aggressive easy monetary policy. Observers, both inside and outside of Japan, called for additional policy measures to stimulate the economy in the latter part of 1998.

There was serious concern the economy would go further into a deflation-recession spiral. The government was urged to take emergency actions. On November 13, 1998, the Bank of Japan announced it would undertake open market operations to purchase private commercial paper with maturity less than a year (amounting to 2 trillion yen), and use corporate bonds as collateral. In addition the Bank of Japan announced that it would provide emergency lending up to 3 trillion yen. On November 16, 1998, the Ministry of Finance announced a fiscal stimulus package of 23.9 trillion yen. The stimulus package was the largest in the Japanese history and contained more than 6 trillion yen in personal and corporate income tax cuts and public investment up to 5.7 trillion yen. The package also included lending (without collateral) to small and medium sized enterprises through to Fiscal Investment and Loan Program and a variety of loan guarantees to private banks for lending to small and medium sized enterprises.

The decline in economic activity and the deflationary trend, however, continued for the remainder of 1998 and into January 1999. The call rate was lowered again in February 1999 to a target level of 0.15 percent and Governor Hayami indicated that a zero interest rate target was also acceptable if warranted by market conditions. Short-term interest rates declined to almost zero in several days. The "zero interest rate policy" became a hallmark of the Bank of Japan policy in 1999. Governor Hayami noted (first at a press conference on April 13, 1999), however, that the commitment to a zero interest rate policy would only be maintained until the deflationary concerns subsided.

One argument against this policy is that such "extreme" measures should only be reserved as a last weapon against a true deflation, of say price deflation of more than 10 percent per annum. In 1998 and 1999 the CPI inflation rate was around 0.0 percent. The decline in real GDP was far from that experienced during the depression of the 1930s and zero percent inflation was far from serious deflation. The conditions may not have required the "extreme" measures adopted by the Bank of Japan in 1999. However, economic conditions at the time did not indicate that monetary policy was especially expansionary. A strong argument could be made that the Bank of Japan should have attempted to be more expansionary, perhaps by broadening open market purchases to medium- and longer-term maturity assets and other means.

The Bank of Japan was operating under difficult conditions. The Bank was operating in an unprecedented environment of deflation and zero short term interest rates. At the same time, the Bank was trying to develop an internal working framework under the 1998 Bank of Japan Law. Under the new Law, independence from the government was secured, so that in principle, the governor and the Policy Board had the ability to formulate policy without fear of being dismissed on the basis of their decisions and opinions. The new legal environment should have reduced "pressure" from the government to take (or not to take) certain actions.

However, some regard the policy changes in 1998 and 1999 as a response to outside pressure, despite the new legal independence of the Bank of Japan. The decision to lower the call rate on September 9, 1999, occurred only several days after the Japan–U.S. Finance Ministers' meeting, at which central bank officials were present. It was reported in the media that the United States had asked for additional stimulus measures during the meeting. (*Nihon Keizai Shinbun*, September 10, 1998). On September 14, 1999, the minutes of the July 28 Policy Board meeting were released. Although additional measures to relax monetary policy were under discussion, the majority of the Board adopted a status quo position. What changed between July and September? The deflationary concern intensified over the summer. On September 11, 1998, the quarter-to-quarter GDP growth rate of the second quarter of 1998 was reported to be −0.8 percent. The yen finally began to appreciate in September, after a long period of depreciation (about 120 in July 1997 to 145 in August 1998).

In November 1998 the Bank of Japan provided more liquidity to the market by increased purchases of commercial paper. The timing of this policy coincided with the announced fiscal stimulus package. The policy coordination between the Ministry of Finance and the Bank of Japan was evident.

Prior to the lowering the call rate in February 1999, the Bank of Japan was under strong political pressure to ease policy further. At the end of January 1999, U.S. Treasury Secretary Rubin asked the Bank of Japan to consider monetizing long-term government bonds. Cabinet Secretary Nonaka and Economic Planning Agency Minister Sakaiya shortly afterward applied similar pressure. The lowering of the call rate from 0.25 to 0.15 percent in February can be regarded as a response to enor-

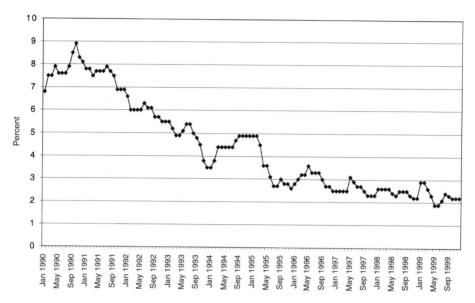

Figure 6.3
Long-term prime lending rate: January 1990 to December 1999. Source: Bank of Japan.

mous pressure from outside; however, it was in all likelihood also the correct policy. (*Nihon Keizai Shinbun*, February 13, 1998, p. 3.)

6.6   Short-Run Monetary Policy Challenge: Providing Liquidity at Zero Interest Rates

With nominal interest rates just above zero percent, further interest rate declines are not possible and monetary stimulus through the interest-rate expenditure channel is no longer effective. Low interest rates, however, did not necessarily indicate easy monetary policy in Japan and the survey results, shown in figure 5.5, indicated that Japanese enterprises viewed credit conditions as "severe" from late 1997 through the first half of 1999. Moreover a related question in the *Tankan* survey reported that corporate enterprises in Japan viewed financial conditions as becoming successively tighter after mid-1997 despite historically low interest rates. Further, real long-term prime lending rates (prime rate adjusted for wholesale price inflation) were high at about 4 percent and had remained essentially unchanged since mid-1995 despite attempts at monetary ease. High real rates reflected the fact that the decline in the nominal long-term prime rate (figure 6.3) was more than matched by the decline in the WPI (figure 2.2).

The Bank of Japan responded to the continuing slump by attempting to increase liquidity, partly by direct purchases of commercial paper in the open market but seemingly without success. How does a central bank provide further stimulus and liquidity when interest rates are virtually zero?

Bank of Japan Credit to the Corporate Sector

The main quantitative response by the Bank of Japan was reflected by changes in the composition of its balance sheet with explicit moves to expand credit to the corporate sector. The Bank of Japan in 1998 and 1999 introduced three new measures for money market operations "in consideration of the risk of the severe financing conditions of Japanese firms intensifying toward the end of calendar 1998 and the end of fiscal 1998 (March 1999)." (Bank of Japan 1999b, p. 66). In other words, the Bank of Japan attempted to ease the credit crunch by direct injections of liquidity into the corporate sector.

The first decision in this regard, at the Monetary Policy Meeting on November 13, 1998, was to expand the size of commercial paper operations in its day-to-day market operations. For this purpose, the scope of eligible commercial paper was expanded to include issues maturing within one year from the day following the Bank's purchase (formerly only three months) and the eligibility evaluation process was shortened. The second decision, also in November 1998, established a new temporary lending facility to support firms' financing activities. This facility refinanced 50 percent of the increase in loans provided by each financial institution during October and December 1998. Japanese government bonds were accepted as collateral, as well as certain private corporations' debt obligations—bills including commercial paper, corporate bonds, and loans on deeds. The third decision, taken in February 1999, established a new market operations scheme utilizing corporate debt obligations as eligible collateral. The Bank, through a bidding process, purchases bills issued by private financial institutions against pooled collateral solely composed of corporate bonds and loans on deeds.

Bank of Japan Aggregate Credit Creation

The logic of these measures was to ensure that liquidity and credit found its way into the corporate sector. But all of these measures, if pursued in tandem, should have expanded the Bank of Japan's balance sheet, eventually increasing bank reserves, base money and aggregate credit in the financial system. Table 6.2 shows the Bank of Japan's balance sheet as of March 1999 (end of the 1998 fiscal year), and the change in composition of assets from the previous year, and as of November 1999. The Bank's balance sheet declined by over 12 percent over the course of the fiscal year, with every main component falling except for loans to the Deposit Insurance Corporation (which rose 3.7 times). This net decline masks considerable volatility, however, as net assets rose sharply in the latter part of 1998 (total assets rose 28 percent in calendar year 1998) but declined sharply during the first quarter of 1999. The Bank of Japan argued that the rapid expansion of its balance sheet in calendar 1998 reflected an "extremely easy" (Bank of Japan 1999b, p. 71) monetary stance taken as a policy to avert deflation and its response to the sluggish economy and the heightened concern about the financial system.

The Bank's "dual operations" are partly responsible for the volatility in its balance sheet. This consisted of providing longer term funds (expanding Bank of Japan assets) to ease pressure on term interest rates, while also absorbing excess funds by selling bills issued to itself (expanding Bank of Japan liabilities). This essentially injects longer-term funds into the financial system, while absorbing short-term funds, and expands the balance sheet on both the asset and liability sides. As a result of "dual" operations, the Bank's total assets increased significantly until the end of 1998.

Early in 1999, however, total assets fell below the previous year's level. This was partly due to technical factors. The Bank implemented fewer "dual" operations, essentially reversing its earlier operations and leading to a decline in both assets and liabilities. In February 1999 the Bank started Finance Bill operations by selling Finance Bills under repurchase agreement. These operations absorbed funds from the money market. Unlike selling bills outright (that increase the liabilities of the Bank), however, Finance Bill repurchase operations decrease assets since the Bank sells Financial Bills from its existing holdings (Bank of Japan 1999b, p. 70).

The worrisome aspect of the contraction in the Bank of Japan's assets in early 1999, however, is that the monetary base declined. The data in table 6.2 indicate a continued contraction in the Bank of Japan balance sheet through November 1999. This fall in assets—including base money—is not simply a technical issue in the way monetary operations

Table 6.2
Changes in principal asset and liability items on the bank's balance sheet (in million yen)

	End of September 1998	Percentage change from previous year	End of December 1998	Percentage change from previous year	End of March 1999	Percentage change from previous year	End of November 1999	Percentage change in previous December
Assets								
Bills purchased (including CP)	10.3	(2.2 times)	13.7	(44.4)	5.2	(−51.2)	8.3	(−39.4)
JGSs in custody (borrowed through repo operations)	4.4	(—)	5.0	(2.2 times)	3.9	(−36.4)	5.0	(0.0)
JGSs (including FBs)	48.9	(7.3)	52.0	(9.8)	49.3	(−6.4)	45.2	(−13.1)
Loans to the Deposit Insurance Corporation	1.0	(3.5 times)	8.0	(27.4 times)		(3.7 times)	2.4	(−70.0)
Total, including other items	78.4	(38.6)	91.2	(27.7)	79.7	(−12.8)	72.7	(−20.1)
Liabilities and capital								
Bills sold	12.8	(6.4 times)	19.6	(3.8 times)	10.0	(−50.7)	2.4	(−87.8)
JGSs borrowed (through repo operation)	4.4	(—)	5.0	(2.2 times)	3.9	(−36.4)	5.0	(0.0)
Current deposits	5.7	(44.3)	4.4	(24.4)	6.2	(5.9)	4.9	(11.4)
Banknotes issued	48.7	(9.4)	53.9	(2.2)	51.3	(4.7)	50.7	(−9.3)
Total, including other items	78.4	(38.6)	91.2	(27.7)	79.7	(−12.8)	72.9	(−20.1)

Note: Figures in parentheses are changes from a year earlier, in percent except as noted.

are conducted (alternative assets being bought and sold), but a sharp decline in the demand for reserves by the banking system that is not being counteracted by the Bank of Japan.

Ineffectiveness of Policy and Accumulation of Excess Reserves

But would more aggressive actions by the Bank of Japan have increased liquidity in the financial system when interest rates were virtually zero and a liquidity trap threatened? The Policy Board decided in its February 1999 meeting to provide "more ample funds" to the market, as well as lower interest rates, and instructed Bank of Japan money managers to inject 500 billion yen of excess reserves into the banking system. This figure was gradually doubled to 1 trillion yen. Ueda (1999b), writing in late September 1999, stated that the Financial Markets Department followed the Board directive and tried daily to inject about one trillion yen (about $9.4 billion) in excess reserves into the financial system in addition to the four trillion yen in required reserves. What actually occurred, however, was that most of this amount (75 percent in early September 1999) ended up in the Bank of Japan accounts of nonbank short-term money-market brokers (*tanshi*). These reserves are not counted in the monetary base. The *tanshi* could not sell these funds to banks, an indication that additional liquidity was not demanded by the banking system.

Okina (1999a) pointed out, in another explanation and defense of Bank of Japan policy, that banks were contributing to money supply growth by purchasing government bonds and other assets instead of providing new loans to businesses or consumers. He argued that banks were simply reluctant to lend, given their concern over capital adequacy ratios and the lack of profitable projects and creditworthy borrowers. He concluded that the Bank of Japan, by lowering interest rates to zero, was not able to be more expansionary in its policy stance. Others at the Bank of Japan reiterated this logic. Inoue (1999), for example, stated that keeping interest rates very close to zero "is all we can reasonably hope for at present."

Extending the Instruments of the Bank of Japan and Solvency of the Central Bank

Given the limitations of providing excess reserves to the market, why didn't the Bank of Japan pursue a more aggressive approach in extending credit using longer-term credit instruments? The main concern appears to have been the potential for a deteriorating balance sheet. Problems could arise, for example, if its "bridge loans" to the Deposit Insurance Corporation (used to facilitate bank restructuring) were not fully repaid. The Bank of Japan may incur some losses from direct loans (e.g., Yamaichi) or share subscriptions (e.g., Nippon Credit Bank and Tokyo Kyodo Bank) to certain financial institutions. The Bank argues, however, that credit risk is not an issue with respect to its loans to the Deposit Insurance Corporation, because repayment is ensured by insurance premiums paid by banks and/or is guaranteed by the government (Bank of Japan 1999b, p. 72). Credit risk associated with the Bank's purchase of corporate debt obligations also appears small because these are purchased from financial institutions under repurchase agreements. The purchase of long-term assets, however, exposes the Bank to risk of capital losses if the instruments are sold before maturity.

At the end of March 1998, the Bank of Japan faced a dilemma: either show its deficits for the fiscal year or change the rule for special reserves from lending losses. Due to the rapid rise of "special Bank of Japan loans" to help finance bank restructuring and closures and provide liquidity to the economy, the assets of the Bank of Japan had increased sharply. At the end of March 1998, the Bank of Japan's balance sheet showed total assets of 91.5 trillion yen—an increase of 50 percent over the previous year.

One-third of the increase was due to "liquidity support"—either due to direct special Bank of Japan loans to defunct financial institutions (i.e., Yamaichi Securities and Hokkaido Takushoku Bank, which both failed in November 1997 at a cost of 3.2 trillion yen) or due to an increase in the purchase of bills, including corporate commercial paper (5.2 trillion yen). Commercial paper was bought from city banks and contributed to a rise in the money supply by increasing reserves, with the objective of alleviating the credit crunch.

Special loans were provided without collateral, so the Bank of Japan established a self-imposed (internal) rule, setting aside special reserves for possible losses in this category of loans. At March 1998, ordinary accounting of the Bank of Japan would have shown that the Bank of Japan made losses, primarily due to special loans to the two institutions. At this point, however, the Bank of Japan changed its policy on the loan-loss reserve ratio, so that its special loans to Hokkaiko Takushoku were only required to be backed by a 10 percent reserve ratio. This avoided a situation that the Bank would show losses from the operation.

As special loans have been provided to large problem institutions—institutions such as Hokkaido Takushoku, Yamaichi, Long-Term Credit Bank, and Nippon Credit Bank—the likelihood increased that the Bank of Japan might suffer serious losses. In principle, the Deposit Insurance Corporation would repay these loans once funds from the sales of assets of these problem institutions were realized. Therefore losses from special loans were only possible if its arrangements with the Deposit Insurance Corporation were breached and the sale of assets did not cover the special loans from the Bank of Japan. However, the Bank of Japan would suffer losses in any case from its subscription to equities of troubled institutions that subsequently failed. For example, in April 1997 Nippon Credit Bank received injections of new capital from the Bank of Japan and other financial institutions as a part of its restructuring plan reflecting the traditional convoy system. This capital became worthless upon Nippon Credit Bank's nationalization by the Financial Supervision Agency in November 1998. Similarly the Bank of Japan subscription to Midori Bank shares—as an arrangement for the failed Hyogo Bank—also became total losses when it was merged with Hanshin Bank.

The balance sheet problem of the Bank of Japan clearly needs to be addressed once the immediate banking and liquidity crisis situation is resolved. The Bank of Japan allayed some of these concerns by emphasizing that it provided liquidity to financial institutions using private firms' debt obligations as the operation instrument or collateral "only after the Bank has thoroughly assessed the creditworthiness of the debtor firm." (Bank of Japan 1999b, p. 72). The *Annual Review* also explained that the creditworthiness of the financial institution was "always used as a backup guaranteeing the safety of any debt obligation held by the Bank." (Bank of Japan 1999b, p. 72). With respect to loans to the Deposit Insurance Corporation, the *Annual Review* noted that credit risk is not an issue because repayment of the loans was ensured by insurance premiums paid by banks and/or was guaranteed by the government. Nonetheless, the Bank of Japan expressed concern that a substantial rise in Deposit Insurance Corporation loans or their becoming a permanent fixture (as opposed to a bridging loan) could impair the Bank's financial soundness and therefore "strongly requested the DIC to minimize its borrowing from the Bank." (Bank of Japan 1999b, p. 72).

Without a serious concern over default risk, why would the Bank of Japan not further expand its balance sheet by additional asset purchases and credit extensions? Other instruments remained to inject liquidity into the economy. For example, the Bank of Japan could have more aggressively increased its purchases of long-term government bonds from the market (as it was considering at the end of 1999). One legal issue is that Japan's Fiscal Law prohibits the Bank of Japan from purchasing new bond issues directly from the Ministry of Finance. The law does allow, however, for the Bank of Japan to purchase long bonds issued one year or more in the past in the secondary market which it had done on occasion.

One objection to this practice might be that central banks in principle should not risk capital losses associated with long-term debt instruments. This seems a small risk, however, given that the Bank could hold the bonds to maturity and that its operating profits are in any case transferred to the government. Many central banks take positions in longer-term government debt instruments. The Federal Reserve System in the United States, for example, undertook significant purchases of long-term government bonds in the early 1950s in an attempt to influence the yield curve as part of an "operation twist" policy. Indeed, the United States pressured Japan to expand the money supply in February 1999 (when the market pushed up long-term interest rates), and Treasury Secretary Rubin reportedly suggested that the Bank of Japan should monetize government bond issues.

The idea at the time was rebuffed by the Japanese authorities because of concerns that such a policy would have an adverse impact on the credibility of the monetary policy and the Bank of Japan. In particular, Bank of Japan officials argued that the government bond rating could be adversely affected if the government issues yet more debt (runs larger fiscal deficits) in response to Bank of Japan purchases. Okina, writing while serving as Director of the Bank of Japan Institute for Monetary and Economic Studies, likened the process to introducing a drug into the economy and that it might be very difficult to stop if the government "came to accept such indulgence." (Okina 1999b, p. 193).

In theory, greater purchases of government debt might provide an incentive for politicians to spend more (e.g., Glick and Hutchison, 2000). This result is based on a government that wants to increase government expenditures to the point where additional expenditures accelerate inflation to an undesirable range. If monetary finance lowers these costs, then the government would tend to increase expenditures, all other factors equal. But the circumstances in Japan at the end of the 1990s were not "normal"; that is, other factors were not "equal." The country was in deep recession and experiencing deflation. The explicit policy of the government was to expand spending in a series of fiscal stimulus packages. Under these circumstances there was little reason to think that an explicitly temporary rise in Bank of Japan purchases of government debt would lead to permanent rise in either government expenditure or inflation.[2] It would increase the Bank of Japan balance sheet and expand base money; however, it would also help provide a monetary stimulus to the economy.[3]

Some Japanese politicians and government officials argued the Bank of Japan should have purchased more long-term government bonds. Cabinet Secretary Nonaka, for example, lobbied for the Bank of Japan to directly purchase government debt issues, clearly illustrating that the central bank was exposed to political pressure despite the new Bank of Japan Law. Some suspected that these pressures resulted in the policy decision of February 12, 1999, to lower the call rate to "as low a level as possible."

A Policy Mistake by the Bank of Japan?

The Bank of Japan may have made a policy mistake in 1999 and early 2000 by not following a more expansionary policy, even if that were to imply less conventional measures such as purchases of long-term government debt. The minutes from the February 24, 2000, Monetary Policy Meeting noted the "weak" year-to-year growth of the money stock (M2 + CDs) of only 2.6 percent in January 2000 (unchanged from December 1999). Year-to-year base money growth was 7.3 percent for February 2000. Virtually zero nominal interest rates were not particularly low when measured in real terms (adjusted for inflation), and were not effective in stimulating the economy. The risks associated with an aggressive move toward monetary expansion—capital losses, credit risk, and bad fiscal incentives—also appeared small at the time. Credit risks were downplayed in the official publications of the Bank

---

2. The experience of the government's approach to dealing with the large deficits that arose after 1973 supports this review (Cargill and Hutchison 1997).

3. Of course, the government needs to meet its long-term "dynamic budget constraint" by either substantially reducing budget deficits or running surpluses in the future after the economy returns to a normal growth path. Further, expansionary fiscal and monetary policies are not a substitute for ongoing structural reforms that are designed to increase efficiency, competitiveness, and raise long-term growth prospects for Japan.

of Japan, and in testimony by Bank officials to the Diet. Capital losses on long-term assets, on the other hand, could have been a problem, but only if Bank of Japan were to sell its holdings before maturity. Perhaps the weakest empirical support is for the view that purchases of term government debt by the Bank of Japan—in a move toward greater monetary stimulus—would lead to a form of dependence by the government and Diet on monetary finance for future budget deficits. The likely benefits of a more aggressive monetary policy, by contrast, were substantial: faster monetary growth, provision of direct credit to firms, and a needed stimulus to the economy.

Conservatism is usually touted as a desirable feature of central bank management as it generally contributes to lower secular inflation. However, formal independence of the Bank of Japan was acquired only recently following enactment of the new central banking law. In this new institutional setting, Bank of Japan officials may have been concerned that their reputation as a conservative (inflation-conscious) central bank would be jeopardized if they had followed a more aggressively expansive monetary policy in the late 1990s and early 2000 despite continued recession and price deflation. Bank officials' desire to succeed in their first major move since enactment of the new central banking law may have made them reluctant to take steps that were uncertain in terms of their ultimate effects on the economy. The irony is that the Bank of Japan became independent at the very time (prolonged recession, deflation and evidence of a liquidity trap) when virtually any policy would have had highly uncertain effects. This may have led officials to follow an unnecessarily "conservative" or timid policy stance. One interpretation of these events is that the Bank found itself in an "independence trap"—following policies that would work in normal times, but that were too restrictive for the situation faced by Japan.

6.7 Long-Run Monetary Policy Challenges: Should the Bank of Japan Adopt an Inflation Target?

Benefits of Inflation Targeting

As explained in chapter 5, inflation targeting has been adopted in several industrial countries including United Kingdom, Sweden, Canada, Australia, and New Zealand since 1990. South Korea, a newly industrialized economy, also adopted inflation targeting in 1997. These countries adopted the inflation targeting policy in order to establish a clear objective of monetary policy and, in some cases, make newly independent central banks accountable. Although exact reasons that prompted these countries to adopt the inflation targeting policy vary from country to country, the result of introducing inflation targeting has been regarded as a success. (See Bernanke et al. 1999 for details of inflation targeting.)

Our view is that the circumstances prevailing in Japan in the late 1990s were consistent with the introduction of an inflation-targeting regime. Others have also reached this conclusion (e.g., see Posen 1998, 1999, and Svensson 1999). Two goals of inflation targeting may be identified in the context of the Japanese situation. First, it would raise inflation expectations in deflationary circumstances. If these expectation changes occurred before reinforcing actual inflation developments, this policy would be judged a success. Second, it would help the Bank of Japan anchor long-run inflation expectations and fend off political pressure. As the new Bank of Japan has to deal with politicians, the inflation target is a transparent way to establish a clear goal, deviations from which would need to be explicitly negotiated with legislators.

An inflation-targeting framework for formulating policy may be considered as targeting directly the final objective, allowing flexibility in the short-run policy instruments (interest rates and central bank money) to achieve the objective. If the central bank were credible, then announcement of the explicit range of an inflation target would have a positive impact on the economic performances by stabilizing inflation and wage growth around the announced target. The monetary policy of the Bank of Japan could also be expected to become more flexible and proactive since it would have an easier time explaining its decisions in the context of an objective that is clear and numerically given. Changes in the policy measures, if necessary, would not damage credibility of the Bank, so long as they are explained in the context of a concrete, stationary target.

An inflation target would define the perimeter of independence for the Bank of Japan. Instrument independence would be secured, once the Bank is committed to an objective of inflation target. The Bank of Japan would benefit from the degree of freedom in choosing instruments, while the other institutions of policy making, including the Diet and the government, could only hold the Bank of Japan responsible if results were not consistent with the announced target. The media cannot expect or blame other institutions putting "pressure" on the

Bank of Japan to take particular policy instruments, as instrument independence is defined clearly.

If the Bank of Japan had followed an inflation-targeting regime in 1997 to 1999, say targeting CPI inflation in a range between 1 and 3 percent, it would have pursued an even more expansionary stance than that actually followed. Continued declines in the deflator would have triggered a stronger policy response than the relatively passive stance than was actually pursued by the Bank of Japan.

On the surface, our argument appears consistent with Krugman's (1999) proposal that the Bank of Japan should deliberately have raised inflation expectations. However, our argument is that stability of inflation expectations is an important long-run objective, not a temporary quick fix to recession and deflation. This argument is articulated in detail in chapter 5. Nonetheless, it seems clear that introducing an inflation targeting regime in the circumstances of the late 1990s would necessarily have induced the Bank of Japan to follow a more expansionary policy stance. This would have helped stop the vicious cycle of expected deflation, recession, high real interest rates, and the increasing debt-burden on borrowers.

The short-run benefits of targeting a low positive rate of inflation would stimulate the economy through three channels. A positive rate of inflation would lower the real interest rate (nominal interest rate minus the inflation rate) and stimulate investment. Since the nominal interest rate is close to zero and cannot be negative (otherwise, individuals and businesses would hoard cash), deflation increases the real interest rate. The real interest rate will only be lowered at this point by stopping deflation. Second, stopping deflation is also important because deflation increases the real value of nominal debt. Increasing the real cost of debt repayment by deflation made the problems of real estate and construction companies, which borrowed heavily from banks, especially difficult. Deflation over the 1997 to 1999 period contributed to the real burden of debt and increased the number of bankruptcies and size of the nonperforming loan problem Third, lower real interest rates would likely stimulate consumption by accelerating the purchase of large consumer durables.

An announcement effect may take place as long as the target framework is clear and understandable to the public, following the adoption of the inflation target. The adoption of a 1 to 3 percent target in Japan would likely raise the inflation expectations of the public. This would in turn stimulate more consumption and investment expenditure, and the expectation of 1 to 3 percent inflation will be self-fulfilled. The benefit of inflation targeting may be realized even before all the right policy measures run their course.

After the crisis of the 1990s, the Bank of Japan faced long-term operational objectives. In the new Law, the Bank of Japan is clearly required to pursue "price stability" and "maintenance of an orderly financial system." These can be regarded as final policy objectives. However, the Law does not define "price stability." An inflation-targeting framework would clarify the intension and objective of Bank of Japan policy, and enhance its accountability. The intention and objective of Bank of Japan policy would become clearer, and its accountability enhanced. In this context, an inflation target would also help stabilize long-run inflation expectations by insulating the central bank from direct political pressure. Under an inflation target the central bank is judged and is accountable to a measurable final objective, and is given the freedom to use the appropriate instruments to achieve that objective.

Implementing Inflation Targeting

Several practical difficulties emerge, however. One problem is the instrument to generate inflation. Another problem is which price index to target. Exactly how Japanese inflation could have been pushed up in the late 1990s is not entirely clear and there was the risk that, following an announced target, credibility of the Bank of Japan may have been hurt if it had not been achieved. The target CPI should be a modified CPI to exclude those items that are not under the control of the Bank of Japan (e.g., energy-related prices and food prices).

A second problem is the credibility of announcement. How would the private sector be convinced of the ability of the Bank of Japan to achieve the target? This can be achieved by the New Zealand style commitment, in that failure to meet the target is the central bank governor's responsibility and is formally reviewed. These problems notwithstanding, the inflation-targeting framework may have been the best policy approach for the new Bank of Japan to adopt in the late 1990s and for policy stability in the medium run.

Third, a particular price index must be chosen. For the purpose of inflation targeting, The CPI is commonly used because it is compiled outside the Bank and is well known by the public. The historical, or past, numbers of the CPI are not regularly revised, and changes in a basket render the continuity of the index questionable. However, as the inflation rate goes, possible discontinuity is a one-time phenomenon. Although the GDP deflator is more comprehensive than the CPI, it takes longer to compile, and it is frequently revised. The Japanese CPI is reliable enough to be used for targeting.

The CPI inflation has a well-known upward bias, however. First, the quality of some goods improves every year. Many features of consumer durables, such as TVs, videos, washing machines, and refrigerators, improve over time. Automobiles certainly improve in their reliability and options, and medical commodities and services have likewise improved in quality. Shiratsuka (1995a, b) estimated the price bias due to quality changes in automobiles and personal computers. Some significant quality improvements are taken into account in measuring inflation, but most quality adjustment is not measured properly in the current CPI.

Moreover the CPI basket in Japan is revised only periodically. New goods, such as mobile phones and personal computers, are not included in the consumption basket in Japan. New goods tend to have rapid quality improvement and price declines even without quality adjustment. The upward bias due to a lack of quality adjustment becomes aggravated by not including these new goods. Therefore, if the CPI is properly measured taking into account quality adjustments, the CPI inflation rate would be lower than the currently measured rate by one to two percentage points. When we refer to zero inflation, it is zero inflation in the quality-adjusted inflation rate, or a 1 to 2 percentage point measured inflation.

Shiratsuka (1999) estimates that the overall bias in the CPI at about 0.90 percentage point per year based on some "bold" assumptions. Nonetheless, it seems safe to assume that 1 percent measured inflation rate actually means that the economy is virtually at price stability. Similarly Boskin et al. (1997) reported a 1.1 percentage point bias for the U.S. CPI.

In a different dimension, the CPI also includes items that are out of the central bank's control. When the central bank is accountable to inflation targeting, it only makes sense that the Bank is not required to neutralize supply shocks. If the straight CPI is used, then the central bank should not be responsible for sudden changes that originate from supply side shocks. Instead, a core CPI, exclusive of first-round energy and food prices, can be calculated, and that can be used for targeting.

Fourth, either the price level or the rate of inflation must be chosen as the target. Price-level targeting means that monetary policy aims at long-run price stability. It prevents the so-called base drift. An unexpected inflation has to be countered by deflation of the same degree later. (Svensson 1999 argues for price-level targeting). Inflation rate targeting, by contrast, often aims at a mild positive inflation and treats past price shocks as by-gones. The price level drifts upward over time. Some argue for benefits of mild inflation, 2 to 4 percent. When the wage is rigid downward, then mild inflation is needed to achieve changes in relative prices reflecting differences in technological progress among different sectors, or reflecting demand shifts.

However, economists differ in their opinions on costs of mild inflation (e.g., below 5 percent). Inflation, however low, has tax effects on those who hold fixed nominal assets, including cash. Mild inflation also requires resources to change prices over time and will likely result in "tax bracket creep" if the tax structure is not indexed to the inflation rate. Higher inflation causes people to use their time on activities to shorten the holding period of nominal assets. Those who advocate mild inflation argue that the cost of mild inflation is small, while the cost of deflation is large. People who advocate mild inflation also emphasize the danger of deflation. Since the nominal interest rate cannot go negative (otherwise, people hoard cash), the deflation rate sets the floor on the real interest rate (which is equal to the sum of the deflation rate and the nominal interest rate).

A fifth technical issue is the choice between a point target or a range. When the inflation-target framework is employed, it can be announced to be a point target or range target. For example, a target can be announced as 2 percent with a plus/minus 1 percent tolerance range. Alternatively, it can be announced as a range between 1 and 3 percent. Those who prefer a point target argue that both the will of the central bank and the expectation of the market to keep the inflation rate near the target are stronger. At the technical level, the difference can be understood as the form of central bank loss function.

These are a few of the practical issues associated with inflation targeting. Other issues include the transition period as the economy adjusts from one monetary regime to another, who sets the target, and how strict will be the accountability for the central bank to achieve the target. These issues are discussed in detail in Bernanke et al. (1999).

Arguments against Inflation Targeting

There are a number of critics of the inflation targeting proposal, not least from Bank of Japan representatives (see Okina 1999a; Ueda

1999b). One argument is that the Bank of Japan Law (Article 2) clearly states that the objective of the Bank is price stability. Why would the Bank of Japan need an explicit numerical inflation target? The problem is that Article 2 of the Bank of Japan Law states that price stability is an objective without giving a precise definition. A clear, numerical target would help achieve accountability for an independent Bank of Japan.

A second argument is that it is difficult to find a good measure of inflation. However, this problem has been addressed by many central banks that have adopted inflation targeting. The CPI serves this purpose, with a proviso that the central bank would not be held responsible for the portion of CPI that moves extraordinarily due to energy prices or primary goods prices. The Bank of Japan could commit to an inflation target of, say, 1 to 3 percent (or 2 percent plus/minus 1 percent) to be achieved over a two-year period. The Bank of Japan would be solely accountable for achieving this objective but would be given a free hand in choosing the instruments to achieve that goal.

A third argument advanced is that there is no credible instrument to achieve the inflation target in a deflationary environment when the interbank interest rate is at zero. Perhaps some effect would occur with the announcement of an inflation target, but this argument holds that long-term credibility of the central bank would likely be damaged. As discussed above, however, there are effective policy instruments to stimulate monetary growth and achieve the inflation target even if interest rates are at the zero-level floor. In the extreme, the Bank of Japan could purchase any asset—say, foreign exchanges, long bonds (in the secondary market), stocks, land, and others—to expand monetary base. There may also be more moderate options. Inflation targeting is credible if the Bank broadens the instruments that are available.

A fourth argument against introducing inflation targeting in Japan is that there is no recent precedent of introducing this type of regime during a deflationary episode—lessons from successful inflation-targeting regimes in other industrial countries may therefore not be applicable to Japan under present circumstances. However, even in the countries that initially sought to lower inflation, the target was sometimes overachieved, that is, the actual inflation rate became lower than the target floor. Central banks in these circumstances moved to relax policy so as to raise inflation back within the range. Another example is the Swedish central bank that introduced price targeting (zero inflation targeting) at the time of going off the gold standard in 1931 in order to prevent deflation that might have resulted from losing a nominal anchor. The experiment is considered a success, although the period is too short to draw a general conclusion (Berg and Jonung 1999).

A fifth argument raised against inflation targeting is that numerical targets may lead the Bank of Japan to ignore GDP and exchange rates in its policy deliberations and design. There is a large literature, however, on the forward-looking nature of inflation-targeting regimes. Variables such as the exchange rate and GDP movements have important implications to future price movements. Inflation targeting must involve forecasting the inflation rate in the future, and the Bank has to examine whether the current policy stance is consistent with achieving the given target. The central bank has to change the stance of monetary policy by choosing correct instruments, in response to changes in major variables, such as GDP, the exchange rate, and interest rates in other countries.

Counterfactuals

Although history cannot be rewritten, one may wonder what would have happened if the new Bank of Japan Law had included inflation targeting. The Bank of Japan might have taken steps to relax monetary policy earlier than when it did had inflation targeting been adopted in April 1998. For example, the short-term interest rate might have approached zero earlier than February 1999 (Svensson 1999).

One of the virtues of inflation targeting is to establish instrument independence. The political process cannot put any pressure on what monetary policy measure could be taken or what interest rate level the Bank should pursue. Another benefit of having an inflation target, assuming the target floor is positive, is that it will automatically force the Bank of Japan to relax policy when prices are falling below zero. As deflationary pressure had been mounting all through 1998, the inflation targeting may have warned the Bank of Japan in the spring or summer of 1998 that more aggressive policy was required.

On balance, the Japanese monetary authorities would likely have benefited from adopting an inflation target policy. Had inflation targeting been adopted, it is probable that the Bank might have taken relaxing measures earlier than actually taken (September and November 1998, and February 1999) and before political pressure mounted. In any event, there is no scenario in which inflation targeting might have harmed monetary policy in 1998 and 1999.

Given the risks in late 1999, our judgment is that a more aggressive monetary policy and the introduction of a moderate inflation target would have been the best course for the new Bank of Japan. An inflation target would not only have helped stabilize expectations and helped counter deflation in the recession, but it would have also been a useful long-term framework to avoid similar future boom-and-bust cycles. An inflation-target strategy should not be seen as a panacea, however. And there could be risks. There is no historical precedent with introducing an inflation targeting regime during a period of deflation, and only limited experience with introducing a price-level target in the midst of a falling price level. Moreover, introducing an inflation target is not a substitute for substantive measures to alleviate structural problems in the Japanese financial sector.

6.8   Concluding Comments

The monetary and financial authorities in Japan face numerous challenges in the years ahead, both of a short-term and long-term nature. This chapter provides our judgment about the appropriate course of policy under very difficult circumstances. The immediate problems are obvious, mainly putting an end to the nonperforming loan problem, establishing a healthy financial system, and restoring growth and price stability. The solutions to these short-run problems are complex, but there are clear lines of direction to be followed.

The long-run challenges are more subtle, but nonetheless very important. The financial structure in Japan is in transition in response to international competitive pressures and changes in the domestic economy. The Big Bang legislation has accelerated the process. But the way the financial system will eventually look is not entirely clear at this point, and the transition process itself can be tumultuous. The Ministry of Finance, the Bank of Japan, the Financial Supervisory Agency, the Financial Reconstruction Commission, and other parts of the government will be hard pressed to manage the transition in a smooth way and not allow another banking crisis to develop. New procedures and institutions in Japan such as Prompt Corrective Action, greater financial system transparency and an independent financial supervisor are important steps that have been taken to help ensure a smooth transition.

A newly independent Bank of Japan is part of the broader set of financial sector market and institutional reforms, and this institution also needs to define its role. We have argued that inflation targeting will help the Bank of Japan achieve its new and clearly defined mandate of price and financial stability, and simultaneously signal the intention—backed up by concrete actions—to prevent deflation by monetary stimulus. In this case, short-run and long-run objectives are entirely consistent, as are considerations of internal and external "balance." That is, monetary stimulus provided in the context of a rigorous, accountable, transparent, and credible inflation targeting regime would have helped establish price stability, depreciate the value of the yen exchange rate, and move the economy out of recession in the late 1990s.

References

Aoki, Masahiko, and Hugh Patrick, eds. 1994. *The Japanese Main Banking System*. Oxford: Oxford University Press.

Alesina, Alberto, and Lawrence H. Summers. 1993. Central Bank independence and macroeconomic performance: Some comparative evidence. *Journal of Money, Credit, and Banking* 25: 151–62.

Bade, Robert, and Michael Parkin. 1982. Central Bank laws and monetary policy. Unpublished manuscript.

Bank of Japan. 1999a. Monthly Report of Recent Economic and Financial Development. November.

Bank of Japan. 1999b. *Annual Review*.

Bank of Japan. 2000. Monthly Report of Recent Economic and Financial Developments. February.

Barro, Robert, and Robert Gordon. 1983. Rules, discretion, and reputation in a model of monetary policy. *Journal of Monetary Economics* 12: 101–21.

Baumgartner, Josef, Ramana Ramaswamy, and G`ran Zettergren. 1997. Monetary policy and leading indicators of inflation in Sweden. Sveriges Riksbank Arbetsrapport 37 (April).

Benston, George J., and George G. Kaufman. 1997. FDICIA after five years. *Economic Perspectives* (summer): 139–58.

Berg, Claes, and Lars Jonung. 1999. Pioneering price level targeting: the Swedish experience 1931–1937. *Journal of Monetary Economics* 43: 525–51.

Berger, Allen N., and Sally M. Davies. 1998. The information content of bank examinations. *Journal of Financial Services Research* 14: 117–44.

Bernanke, Ben, Thomas Laubach, Frederic Mishkin and Adam Posen. 1999. *Inflation Targeting: Lessons from International Experience*. Princeton, New Jersey: Princeton University Press.

Boskin, Michael, Ellen Dulenberger, Robert Gordon, Zvi Griliches, and Dale Jorgenson. 1997. The CPI commission: Findings and recommendations. *American Economic Review* 87: 78–83.

Burdekin, Richard C. K., and Thomas D. Willet. 1991. Central Bank reform: The Federal Reserve in international perspective. *Public Budgeting and Financial Management* 3: 619–49.

Burdekin, Richard C. K., Clas Wihlborg, and Thomas D. Willett. 1992. Central Bank reform: The Federal Reserve in international perspective. *World Economy* 15: 231–49.

Cargill, Thomas F. 1989. CAMEL ratings and the CD market. *Journal of Financial Services Research* 3: 347–58.

Cargill, Thomas F. 1989. *Central Bank Independence and Regulatory Responsibilities: The Bank of Japan and The Federal Reserve.* Monograph Series in Finance and Economics, Salomon Brothers Center for the Study of Financial Institutions, New York University.

Cargill, Thomas F. 1993a. The Bank of Japan: A dependent but price stabilizing central bank. *Public Budgeting and Financial Management* 5: 131–39.

Cargill, Thomas F. 1993b. Deposit guarantees, nonperforming loans, and the postal savings system in Japan. In *FDICIA: An Appraisal.* Federal Reserve Bank of Chicago.

Cargill, Thomas F. 1995. The statistical association between central bank independence and inflation. *Banca Nazionale Del Lavoro: Quarterly Review* June: 159–72.

Cargill, Thomas F. 1997–98. Can central bank reform solve Korea and Japan's financial problems? *Central Banker* 8: 44–52.

Cargill, Thomas F. 1998a. Financial crisis, reform and prospects for Korea. *Financial Regulator* 3: 36–40a.

Cargill, Thomas F. 1998b. Korea and Japan: The end of the "Japanese Financial Regime." In George Kaufman, ed., *Bank Crises: Causes, Analysis and Prevention.* London: JAI Press.

Cargill, Thomas F. 2000. What Caused Japan's Banking Crisis? In Takeo Hoshi and Hugh Patrick, eds., *Crisis and Change in the Japanese Financial System.* Dordrecht: Kluwer Academic, frothcoming.

Cargill, Thomas F., and Michael M. Hutchison. 1997. The international dimension of macroeconomic policies in Japan. In Michele U. Fratianni, Dominick Salvatore, and Jurgen Von Hagen, eds., *Macroeconomic Policy in Open Economies.* Westport, CT: Greenwood Press.

Cargill, Thomas F., Michael M. Hutchison, and Takatoshi Ito. 1996. Deposit guarantees in Japan: Aftermath of the bubble and burst of the bubble economy. *Contemporary Economic Policy* July: 41–52.

Cargill, Thomas F., Michael M. Hutchison, and Takatoshi Ito. 1997. *The Political Economy of Japanese Monetary Policy.* Cambridge: MIT Press.

Cargill, Thomas F., Michael M. Hutchison, and Takatoshi Ito. 1998. The banking crisis in Japan. In G. Caprio Jr., W. C. Hunter, G. G. Kaufman, and D. M. Leipziger, eds., *Preventing Bank Crises: Lessons from Recent Global Bank Failures.* Washington, DC: World Bank.

Cargill, Thomas F., Michael M. Hutchison, and Takatoshi Ito. 1999. Inflation targeting liquidity traps and the New Bank of Japan. Paper presented at the European Network on the Japanese Economy conference, Oxford, UK, July 30–31.

Cargill, Thomas F., and Thomas. Mayer. 1998. The Great Depression and History Textbooks. *History Teacher* (August): 441–58.

Cargill, Thomas F., and Shoichi Royama. 1988. *The Transition of Finance in Japan and the United States: A Comparative Perspective.* Stanford, CA: Hoover Institution Press.

Cargill, Thomas F., and Naoyuki Yoshino. 1998. Too big for its boots. *Financial Regulator* 3: 39–42.

Cargill, Thomas F., and Naoyuki Yoshino. 2000. The postal savings system, fiscal investment and loan program, and modernization of Japan's financial system. In Takeo Hoshi and Hugh Patrick, eds., *Crisis and Change in the Japanese Financial System*. Dordrecht: Kluwer Academic.

Choy, Jon. 1999. Government reorganization plan advances. Japan Economic Institute, JEI Report 17B (April).

Cole, David C. 1993. The political economy of Korean–U.S. financial relations. *Korean–U.S. Financial Issues*. Washington DC: Korea Economic Institute of America.

Cukierman, Alex. 1996. The economics of central banking. In Wolf Holger, ed., *Macroeconomic Policy and Financial Systems*. New York: Macmillan.

Cukierman, Alex, Steven B. Webb, and Bilin Neyapti. 1993. Measuring the independence of central banks and its effect on policy outcomes. *World Bank Economic Review* 6: 353–98.

Debelle, Guy, and Stanley Fischer. 1994. How Independent Should a Central Bank Be? In J. C. Fuhrer, ed., *Goals, Guidelines, and Constraints Facing monetary Policymakers*. Boston: Federal Reserve Bank of Boston.

Debelle, Guy. 1997. Inflation targeting in practice. IMF Working Paper. March.

Demirguc-Knut, Asli, and Enrica Detragiache. 1998. The determinants of banking crises in developing and developed countries. *IMF Staff Papers*. 45: 81–109.

Economist, 1997. Banking in emerging markets. April 12.

Eijffinger, Sylvester, and Eric Schaling. 1993. Central bank independence in twelve industrial countries. *Banca Nazionale del Lavoro Quarterly Review* 184: 1–41.

Feldman, Robert Alan. 1986. *Japanese Financial Markets: Deficits, Dilemmas, and Deregulation*. Cambridge: MIT Press.

Friedman, Milton, and Anna Jacob Schwartz. 1963. *A Monetary History of the United States*. Princeton, NJ: Princeton University Press.

Glick, Reuven, and Michael M. Hutchison. 1993. Fiscal policy in monetary unions: Implications for Europe. *Open Economies Review* 3: 39–65.

Glick, Reuven, and Michael M. Hutchison. 2000. Banking and currency Crises: How common are twins? In R. Glick, R. Moreno, and M. Spiegel, eds., Financial Crises in Emerging Markets. Cambridge: Cambridge University Press.

Goodhart, Charles, and Dirk Schoenmaker. 1993. Institutional separation between supervisory and monetary agencies. Special Paper 52, London School of Economics Financial Markets Group, April.

Goodhart, Charles, and Dirk Schoenmaker. 1995. Should the functions of monetary policy and banking supervision be separated? *Oxford Economic Papers* 47: 539–60.

Grilli, Vittorio, Donato Masciandaro, and Guido Tabellini. 1991. Political and monetary institutions and public finance policies in the industrial countries. *Economic Policy* 13: 341–92.

Haubrich, Joseph G. 1996. Combining bank supervision and monetary policy. *Economic Commentary*. Federal Reserve Bank of Cleveland. November.

Hoshi, Takeo, and Anil Kashyap. 1999. The Japanese bank crisis: Where did it come from and how will it end? *NBER Macroeconomics Annual 1999*.

Hutchison, Michael M. 1995a. Central bank credibility and disinflation in New Zealand. Federal Reserve Bank of San Francisco. *Weekly Letter*, February 10.

Hutchison, Michael M., and Kathleen McDill. 1999a. Empirical determinants of banking crises: Japan's experience in international perspective. In C. Freeman, ed., *Why Did Japan Stumble? Causes and Cures*. England: Edward Elgar.

Hutchison, Michael M., and Kathleen McDill. 1999b. Are all banking crises alike? The Japanese experience in international perspective. *Journal of the Japanese and International Economies* (December): 155–80.

Hutchison, Michael M., and C. Walsh. 1998a. The output-inflation tradeoff and central bank reform: Evidence from New Zealand. *Economic Journal* 108: 1–23.

Hutchison, Michael M., and Carl Walsh. 1998b. Disinflation in New Zealand. Paper presented at the Banco De La Republica and World Bank conference: Why Is It Important to Reduce Inflation and How to Do It? The International Experience and Lessons for Colombia, Bogota, Colombia, May 4–5.

Inoue, Kengo. 1999. Japan finds the right policy mix. *Wall Street Journal*. March 25.

International Monetary Fund. 1995. The adoption of indirect instruments of monetary policy. IMF Occasional Paper 126 (June).

International Monetary Fund. 1999. *International Capital Markets*. Washington, DC: International Monetary Fund.

Ito, Takatoshi. 1999. Why the Bank of Japan needs an inflation target. *Financial Times*.

Ito, Takatoshi. 2000. The stagnant Japanese economy in the 1990s: The need for financial supervision to restore sustained growth. In Takeo Hoshi and Hugh Patrick, eds., *Crisis and Change in the Japanese Financial System*. Dordrecht: Kluwer Academic.

Ito, Takatoshi, and Kimie Harada. 2000. Japan premium and stock prices: Two mirrors of the Japanese banking crises. Memorandum.

Ito, Takatoshi, and Yuri Nagataki Sasaki. 1998. Impacts of the Basel capital standard on Japanese banks' behavior. NBER Working Paper, No. 6730. September.

Japan Times Office. 1902. *The Act and By-laws of Nippon Ginko (The Bank of Japan)*. Tokyo, Japan.

Kahn, George A., and Klara Parrish. 1998. Conducting monetary policy with inflation targets. *Economic Review (Federal Reserve Bank of Kansas City)* 83: 5–32.

Kaminsky, Graciela, and Carman Reinhart. 1996. The twin crisis: The causes of banking and balance of payments problems. Board of Governors of the Federal Reserve System, International Finance Discussion Papers 544 (March).

Krugman, Paul. 1998. Japan: Still trapped. Mimeo (November), from Paul Krugman web site.

Krugman, Paul. 1999. It's Baaack! Japan's slump and the return of the liquidity trap. *Brookings Papers on Economic Activity* 2: 137–205.

Lee, Chung H. 1992. The government, financial system, and large private enterprises in the economic development of South Korea. *World Development* 20: 187–97.

Lindgren, Carl-Johan, Gillian Garcia, and Matthew I. Saal. 1996. *Bank Soundness and Macroeconomic Policy*. Washington, DC: International Monetary Fund.

Lohmann, Susanne. 1997. Is Japan Special? Monetary Linkages and Price Stability. *Monetary and Economic Studies (Bank of Japan)* 15: 63–79.

Mabuchi, Masaru. The political economy of the MOF reform. Presented at The Japanese Financial System: Restructuring for the Future, Columbia University, October 1–2, 1998.

Mayer, Thomas. 1982. A Case Study of Federal Reserve Policymaking: Regulation Q in 1966. *Journal of Monetary Economics* 10: 259–71.

Maxfield, Sylvia. 1997. *Gatekeepers of Growth: The International Political Economy of Central Banking in Developing Countries*. Princeton, NJ: Princeton University Press.

McCallum, Bennett T. 1996. Inflation Targeting in Canada, New Zealand, Sweden, the United States, and in General. NBER Working Paper No. 5579. May.

McKinnon, Ronald J. 1999. Comments on "monetary policy under zero inflation." *Monetary and Economic Studies* (Bank of Japan) 17: 183–87.

Meltzer, Allan H. 1999. Comments: What more can the Bank of Japan do? *Monetary and Economic Studies* (Bank of Japan) 17: 189–91.

Mikitani, Ryoichi, and Patricia Kuwayama. 1998. Japan's new central banking law: A critical review. Presented at the Japan Economic Seminar, Center on Japanese Economy and Business, Columbia University, September 28.

Milhaupt, Curtis J. 1999. Japan's experience with deposit insurance and failing banks: Implications for financial regulatory design? *Monetary and Economic Studies (Bank of Japan)* 17: 21–46.

Mishkin, Frederic, and Adam Posen, 1997. Inflation targeting: Lessons from four countries. *Economic Policy Review (Federal Reserve Bank of New York)* 3: 9–110.

Montes, Manuel F., and Vladimir V. Popov. 1999. *Asian Crisis Turns Global*. Singapore: Institute for Southeast Studies.

Nakaso, Hiroshi. 1999. Recent banking sector reforms in Japan. *Economic Policy Review (Federal Reserve Bank of New York)* 5: 1–7.

Nihon Keizai Shinbun, September 10, 1998.

Nihon Keizai Shinbun, February 13, 1998.

Okina, Kunio. 1999a. Monetary policy under zero inflation: A response to criticisms and questions regarding monetary policy. *Monetary and Economic Studies* (Bank of Japan) 17: 157–82.

Okina, Kunio. 1999b. Rejoinder to comments made by Professors McKinnon and Meltzer. *Monetary and Economic Studies* (Bank of Japan) 17: 192–97.

Okina, Kunio. 1999c. Monetary policy under zero inflation: How to respond to questions and criticisms of monetary policy. *Kin-yu Kenkyu* (Bank of Japan) August 121–54. (In Japanese)

Packer, Frank. 2000. The disposal of bad loans in Japan: The case of CCPC. In Takeo Hoshi and Hugh Patrick, eds., *Crisis and Change in the Japanese Financial System*. Dordrecht: Kluwer Academic.

Patrick, Hugh T. 1971. The economic muddle of the 1920s. In J. W. Morely, ed., *Dilemmas of Growth in Prewar Japan*. Princeton, NJ: Princeton University Press.

Persson, T., and G. Tabellini, 1993. Designing Institutions for Monetary Stability. Carnegie-Rochester Conference Series on Public Policy, 39 (December)

Posen, Adam S. 1998. *Restoring Japan's Economic Growth*. Washington, DC: Institute for International Economics.

Posen, Adam S. 1999. Nothing to fear but fear (of inflation) itself. *International Economics Policy Briefs*. Washington, DC: Institute for International Economics, October.

Shiratsuka, Shigenori. 1995a. Effects of quality changes on the price index: A hedonic approach to the estimation of a quality-adjusted price index for personal computers in Japan. *Bank of Japan Monetary and Economic Studies* 13: 17–52.

Shiratsuka, Shigenori. 1995b. Automobile prices and quality changes: A hedonic price analysis of the Japanese automobile market. *Bank of Japan Monetary and Economic Studies* 13: 1–44.

Shiratsuka, Shigenori. 1999. Measurement error in the Japanese consumer price index. *Bank of Japan Monetary and Economic Studies*, 17: 69–102.

Svensson, Lars E. O. 1997a. Inflation forecast targeting: Implementing and monitoring inflation targets. *European Economic Review* 41: 1111–46.

Svensson, Lars E. O. 1997b. Optimal inflation contracts, "conservative central banks," and linear inflation contracts. *American Economic Review* 87: 98–114.

Svensson, Lars E. O. 1999 How should monetary policy be conducted in an era of price stability. Presented in the Federal Reserve Bank of Kansas conference, *New Challenges for Monetary Policy*, Jackson Hole, August.

Shionoya, Tsukumo. 1962. *Problems Surrounding the Revision of the Bank of Japan Law*. Nagoya, Japan: Beckhard Foundation.

Suzuki, Yoshio, ed. 1987. *The Japanese Financial System*. Oxford: Clarendon Press.

Takahashi, Tomohiko. 1998. Kaisei Nichigin-ho no igi to kongo no kadai (Significance and Challenges in the Future of the Revised Bank of Japan Law). Nissay Research Institute, Report (September).

Ueda, Kazuo. 1999a. The Bank of Japan's year of freedom. *Wall Street Journal*, April 8.

Ueda, Kazuo. 1999b. The Bank of Japan holds the line. *Wall Street Journal*, September 22.

Ueda, Kazuo. 2000. Causes of Japan's Banking Problems in the 1990s. In Takeo Hoshi and Hugh Patrick, eds., *Crisis and Change in the Japanese Financial System*. Dordrecht: Kluwer Academic.

Wall Street Journal. 1996. "The way a bureaucracy beats back reform says volumes about Japan," by Jathon Sapsford. August 2.

Wall Street Journal. 1997. "Postal savings may prove popular throughout Asia," by Masayoshi Kanabayashi. April 18.

Wall Street Journal. 1999. "Japan intensifies pressure on its major banks to dispose of bad loans by end of fiscal year," by Jathon Sapsford. January 21.

Wall Street Journal. 1999. "Japan's regulators act tough as bank deadline nears," by Jathon Sapsford. February 8.

Walsh, Carl. 1995a. Central Bank Independence and the Costs of Disinflation in the European Community. In B. Eichengreen, J. Frieden, and J. v. Hagen, eds., *Monetary and Fiscal Policy in an Integrated Europe*. Berlin: Springer-Verlag.

Walsh, Carl. 1995b. Is New Zealand's Reserve Bank Act of 1989 an optimal central bank contract? Part I. *Journal of Money, Credit and Banking* 27: 1179–91.

Walsh, Carl. 1998. *Monetary Theory and Policy*. Cambridge MIT Press.

Weinstein, David E. 2000. How bad is the Japanese crisis? Macroeconomic and structure perspectives. In Magnus Blomstrom, Byron Gangnes, and Sumner La Croix, eds., *Japan's Economy in the Twenty-First Century: The Response to Crisis*. Oxford: Oxford University Press.

Index